ADSENSE
NICHE SIT
UNLEASH

THE STEP BY STEP GUIDE TO BUILDING A PROFITABLE THICK ADSENSE WEBSITE – WITH CASE STUDY

BY: JOHN ELDER
MARKETINGFOOL.COM

Adsense Niche Sites Unleashed: The Step By Step Guide To Building A Profitable Thick Adsense Website – With Case Study

By John Elder

Published By Avery & Co. Publishing

New York, NY USA

ISBN 0-9725604-4-0

Second Edition

DISCLAIMER

All material contained in this book is for informational purposes only and is no substitute for professional advice. Neither John Elder, MarketingFool.com, Flatplanet Media, LLC or it's affiliates (collectively referred to as COMPANY) make any guarantees of the tactics or strategies described in this book. Successful use of any tactic or strategy described in this book depends on the specific person, their experience, and their business and marketing ability. COMPANY makes no claims or guarantees regarding income generated from the use of any tactic or strategy described in this book. Reader agrees to indemnify and hold COMPANY harmless from and against any and all claims, demands, liabilities, expenses, losses, damages, attorney fees arising from any and all claims and lawsuits for libel, slander, copyright, and trademark violation as well as all other claims resulting from reading this book. Adsense is a registered trademark of Google.

A Note From The Author

If you find any typos or grammatical errors in this book, they're there for a reason. Some people like searching for them and I aim to please! If you find one and want to let me know, you can contact me at www.marketingfool.com/contact-me

TABLE OF CONTENTS

INTRODUCTION
What To Expect

WELCOME!

Hello, my name is John Elder and I'm The Marketing Fool…

I want to take a moment to thank you for purchasing this eBook and taking the first step toward building a thick site Adsense Empire.

In my opinion, there's no better lifestyle than the online marketing lifestyle. Once you know a few simple skills, there's literally nothing you can't accomplish and no amount of money you can't make.

That's why I built MarketingFool.com and why it's become one of the most popular sites on the Internet for people learning to make money online.

It boggles my mind how quickly we've grown into the vibrant community of like-minded people that we are today. I hope you get a lot out of this ebook, but even more, I hope that you return and join our community.

Because it's everyone coming together to help each other out that makes the site such an enormous success. We're all pulling together to help each other with tips, tricks, and support in building our own online businesses.

And that really makes us unique.

So enjoy this eBook! And if you ever have any questions at all, just head over to MarketingFool.com and hit the contact me link, I'm always just an email away!

WHAT TO EXPECT FROM THIS BOOK

Simply put, I'm going to teach you how I build thick Adsense websites. I'm going to walk you through it step by step, giving you absolutely everything you need in order to start your own profitable Adsense Empire.

But unlike other courses or books out there, I'm not just going to tell you what to do...I'm going to SHOW you what to do by walking you through a real life case study website that actually made lots of money.

We'll be using my old EspressoShack.com website as an example. I built it about a year ago and sold it a few weeks ago on flippa.

While I no longer own the site, I can still show you exactly how I built it, how it made money, how I sold it, and how you can do the exact same thing…over and over and over again.

The site brought in around $3,200 total in about ten months.

That breaks down to:

TEN MONTH INCOME REPORT

Adsense Income:	$856.73
Amazon Affiliate Income:	$641.33
Sold the Site for:	$1,700.00
TOTAL:	$3,198.06

That might not seem like a lot of money, but:

1. It only took me about a week to build the site

2. I did virtually NO marketing or seo linking to the site after I built it.

3. It was less than 150 pages of content.

4. It ran completely on autopilot after it was built; I didn't have to do anything at all to it and the money just kept rolling in.

5. After 10 months or so, I easily sold it on Flippa for $1,700 (there were lots of bidders and the guy that bought it grabbed it for the BIN price before the auction even ended – I probably could have got more for it).

Just think about that for a minute. A website that took about a week to build and no work after that brought in around $3,200 on autopilot.

If you wanted a yearly income of $100,000 how many of those sites would you have to make? Do the math and it comes out to around 32 websites.

Building one website a week, it would take you around 6 months to reach that income level if you did everything yourself.

Start outsourcing the content creation and you could create that many sites in a few weeks! It's all up to you.

Of course, my past success with that site is not indicative of your future success. (My attorney wanted me to say that)

Some sites will pull in more money than others, that's just part of the game. But I'll give you the exact roadmap that I used to build espressoshack.com and you can do the rest.

No Hype Here…

Aren't you tired of Internet marketing hype that promises to teach you how to make millions of dollars online?

I prefer to focus on something more down to earth and I think my thick Adsense sites (that each bring in a few thousand dollars) are something that anyone can do.

QUESTIONS

Before we dive into the meat of the book, I want to make something perfectly clear.

You purchased this book. In my mind, that means you get access to me for any questions you have about the stuff you read here.

I take that very seriously. Making sure that you understand everything you read here and get the most out of this book is important to me, so if you ever have any questions; or if there's something you don't quite understand… I strongly encourage you to email me.

To get a hold of me, just head over to MarketingFool.com and click the Contact link at the top of every page, then fill out the form and send me your questions.

I'll answer as soon as I can, usually within the same day.

I know a lot of Internet Marketing guru types pretend to offer this sort of help, but I actually take it seriously. You'll always be able to get a hold of me.

And if you want to really be a part of our community at MarketingFool.com, I encourage you to join my **members only** section of the site (**www.marketingfool.com/member**).

It's where a ton of us hang out to talk about Internet marketing and share our current money making activities.

There's lots of articles, video's, other case studies of things that I'm doing right now that are working well, and discussions on things that aren't working.

There's a vibrant members forum where you can post questions and get help for virtually every aspect of your businesses.

Check it out at:
http://www.marketingfool.com/member

It's not free, but the cost comes to pennies a day and has a money back guarantee. Would you be willing to spend a few pennies per day to become a part of a community of like minded people dedicated to helping each other's businesses grow online?

In my opinion, it's worth its weight in gold.

But I'm getting off track here… let's dive right in and start learning about building thick Adsense websites!

Before we get started, we need to discuss just a little but of housekeeping.

Throughout this book I'll be talking about my espressoshack.com website and using it as an example.

Like I said earlier, I sold that website and no longer own it, but I've thrown up an exact copy behind a password protected barrier that only people who bought this book can view.

You can access that site at:
http://espressoshack.marketingfool.com

To log in, use:

Username: espresso
Password: shack

The site is virtually identical to the original, except that I've removed the actual adsense ads and replaced them with pictures of ads for obvious reasons.

I encourage you to head over and take a look at that site. Click around on the links and look the whole thing over because I'm going to reference it throughout this eBook.

CHAPTER ONE
The Strategy

Hello good people!

I'm excited to dive in and share my thick site methods with you today!

Unlike most Internet Marketing types out there, I actually practice what I preach and I'm putting my money where my mouth is by walking you through an actual real life case study.

I thought I'd start out by explaining the overall strategy to my thick site Adsense methods, and then dig into the nitty gritty with actual specifics.

I feel like it's good to have a broad overview before we get into specifics, so that's what I'm going to talk about now.

Why An Adsense "Empire"?

Throughout this eBook and at my MarketingFool.com website I often refer to the term "Empire". You could say that it's a running theme for me.

But why?

It's because Adsense is really sort of unique. It's nearly impossible, or at least VERY VERY hard to create a huge income stream by putting Adsense ads on just one website.

One of the characteristics of Adsense is that you need a lot of site traffic to make a lot of money.

People build one website, throw up some Adsense ads, see that those ads are making $2-3 dollars a day (or even $10 a day). And quit in disgust because that's just not enough money.

The trick is to not limit yourself to one website; but rather create dozens, if not hundreds of websites; each earning a few dollars to ten-twenty dollars each.

One website making $3 a day is $90 a month in income…and that's just lousy.

But 100 websites making $3 a day is $9,000 a month in income ($3x100 = $300 a day…$300/day x 30days = $9,000 a month).

All of a sudden, making $3 in ad income on a website doesn't sound so lousy!

So that's why I like to use the word "Empire" to refer to your Empire of dozens of websites.

It's a little cheesy but it really encapsulates the overall theme of what we're doing here and what we're attempting to build, plus it's just fun to build an Empire...

MY THICK SITE STRATEGY

My thick Adsense site strategy is similar to many others that are floating around out on the Internet...but not completely the same.

Most thick site strategies are variations on the same main strategy. It's not really new.

I mean, when you get right down to it; the concept is pretty simple and straight forward;

- Create a website based on a major keyword.

- Create tons of targeted content around that keyword in order to draw in free search engine traffic.

- Monetize the site with Adsense, Amazon affiliate, and cpa offers.

- Rinse and repeat!

But how you implement each of those things is where the art and science of it come in.

Wordpress, HTML, Or Other?

I hand-code my pages using HTML and PHP (a programming language well suited for web development). I do that because it gives me a level of control that's awesome, and also because it makes my sites small and fast loading.

And also, I can cram a bunch of sites onto my web server that way, whereas Wordpress is a massive resource hog and would cost more in web hosting and bandwidth per site.

But most importantly… *it doesn't matter what you use!*

If you're more familiar and comfortable with Wordpress, then certainly use it. It works just fine.

In fact, I've thought about developing a wordpress template that mirrors my thick site design for those of you who like wordpress.

Use what works best for you. I fly with php…but wordpress is much easier for someone just starting out. You can find decent wordpress templates all over the place. Check out my website for recommendations.

How Many Pages Of Content Per Site?

There is no hard and fast rule of thumb that says thick websites are made up of X number of specific pages. It really just depends.

As a good rule of thumb, I like to shoot for around 150 pages per thick site.

But that's really just a starting off point! 150 is around the minimum in my mind.

If you build a thick site with 150 pages and it really takes off; that is, if Google really ranks the site well and people start flooding to your door, then you would probably want to build out the site even more.

So keep that in mind.

But for the purposes of our thick site road map, let's start with 150 pages per site.

What Are Content Pages?

When I say 150 pages, I mean 150 pages of content. You'll also need a contact page, and about page, a privacy policy page, sitemap page, rss feed pages, etc.

Espressoshack.com had around 150 pages of actual content, plus all those other pages.

For each content page, I aim for 500 words minimum, though I like to write 750-1,200 words when I can.

Everyone shoots for 500 words per page. Differentiate yourself as much as you can with longer articles. Google will appreciate it!

Basic Site Layout

My thick sites are all laid out the same, there's a header graphic at the top (make it as nice as you can), with some small contact, about, privacy policy links directly below and horizontal to the header.

Then I usually put a menu on the right hand side with 20-30 links to the main categories of the site, usually brand names.

In the middle of the page I'll start off with an Adsense ad block, followed by the actual 500-1,200 word article.

Directly under that article I'll put an Amazon.com affiliate widget selling whatever item the article is discussing.

Directly under that I'll put links to all the other pages of content that are related to that article.

For instance, if my brand name is Capresso Espresso Machine, and I've written 5 articles about different Capresso Espresso Machines, then the links to each of those articles will go there.

SEO types call this Silo-ing your site. (more on that later).

I make the homepage of each site look a little different, and I'll talk about that as we get into more specifics, but the main content pages pretty much stick to the layout I just described. Here's a picture:

Espresso Shack
Espresso Machines - The Ultimate Guide
Email
Marketing
Made
Easy
$1 Trial
$19/Mo.
Find Out
More
AWeber

Don't worry, in a little while I'm going to direct you to a mockup of the site that I've created online so that you can really dig around and see what the site looks like and how it was designed.

The above picture is just to give you a basic idea of what I'm talking about design-wise.

Content Blueprint

I'll discuss this in more detail later in the book, but to give you an idea of how to build your thick site, think of content like this…

Each thick site you build should be about one broad theme. In this case, espressoshack.com was about espresso machines.

Once you have your theme, choose 20-30 categories related to that theme. In espressoshack.com's case, the categories where brand names of espresso companies.

No matter what product you choose, there's a good chance that you can find 20-30 brands. But if not, you might pick features too.
For espressoshack.com I picked about 20 brand names and three generic feature categories; espresso machines, espresso parts, espresso beans.

You get the idea.

Next, aim to write around 5 articles per category. 5 articles times 20 categories equals 100 pages. Also write one article per category as a sort of introduction to that category.

One intro article per category, at 20 categories equals 20 pages, plus your 100 previous pages and you're already at 120. Add a couple more here and there and you've got your 150 pages.

Piece of cake.

That way you have a nice themed and silo'd website.

Still with me?

Here's an example. One of the categories of espressoshack.com was **Capresso Coffee** (you'll find a link that that on the right side menu of the site.

Within that category I wrote 6 articles, namely:

- Capresso Replacement Parts
- Capresso Infinity Conical Burr Grinder
- Capresso 121.01 Ultima Espresso Machine
- Capresso 303.01 4-Cup Espresso And Cappuccino Machine
- Capresso 115.01 Capresso Cafe Espresso Machine
- Capresso Espresso Machines

The list of those links sits at the bottom of every page of that category.

I'll talk more about the specifics of this later on. Hopefully now you get the broad idea.

So let's dive into the actual specifics.

CHAPTER TWO

Picking a Theme For Your Thick Site

Before you do anything, you need to choose a theme for your website. This can be very important, but it doesn't have to be as difficult as many people would have you believe.

Most books on Adsense websites tend to put a lot of thought and effort into choosing the right website theme. By theme I don't mean a wordpress theme, I mean the overall topic that your website will be about.

In my espressoshack.com website, the theme is obviously "espresso machines".

Keyword Research

Most people put a ton of time, effort, and expense into picking the right theme based on keyword research. They spend hundreds of dollars on keyword research tools in order to analyze the market and find the best keywords.

I'll admit it; I've done that in the past. I've even developed intricate algorithms to analyze the market to discover and determine what the best keywords would be from a mathematical point of view.

But it's all hogwash…it's completely and totally unnecessary!

"But…" people will say, "…you can't pick a niche that is too competitive!"

Of course you can! It doesn't matter, and I'll tell you why.

Let's take espressoshack.com as an example. By any analysis, espresso machines is WAY WAY WAY too competitive.

There are major players in that space who are dominating the search engines for all those major espresso machine keywords.

I couldn't ever hope to get listed at Google in the top ten listings under the keyword "Espresso Machine".

So how did I make so much money with literally no SEO marketing?

Easy; Long Tail Keywords.

Long tail keywords are where most of your traffic is going to come from, and there's NEVER any competition to speak of in that space.

Why? Because the traffic is so small, big name players don't bother optimizing their sites for them.

An example of a long tail keyword for espresso machines is:

"Capresso 303.01 4-Cup Espresso And Cappuccino Machine"

That phrase gets searched for at Google 260 times per month. That's not enough for any major website to bother with.

So what did I do? I built an entire page about that keyword. And I got a handful of visitors a day to that page, all looking for that exact thing.

And since they're looking for that exact thing, guess what they did when they saw an ad for that thing on sale, or an amazon widget selling the actual product at 30% off?

You guessed it; many clicked the ad or outright bought the product from my website.

That's the entire point of this whole strategy and why it works so well.

And that means that you don't have to spend ANY time analyzing keywords to pick your main website theme.

I like to do it by simply making websites about things I like. In this case, I love espresso so I made an espresso machine website.

Some Simple Rules...

There are a few rules to follow when picking a site theme.

FIRST: It must be a product of some sort. Why? Because we monetize the websites with Adsense ads and Amazon widgets selling products.

Your site has to be about something that has advertiser potential. Spyfu.com is a good free resource to use. It will show you how many advertisers are buying adsense ads for any specific keyword.

But you don't really need to research this. You should be picking things that are obviously commercial in nature.

Things like espresso machines, vacuum cleaners, power drills, cooking pots and pans, clothing, jewelry, lawn equipment, etc.

Just about anything commercial will work. If people buy it, then you're probably good to go.

Sometimes when I need ideas for website themes, I'll simply go wander around in Walmart or Target or any other store and find ideas.

Broad is Good…

You want to pick a theme that is fairly broad, like espresso machines because that gives you a ton of things to write about.

The narrower you go with your theme selection, the harder it will be to write a hundred and fifty pages of content.

I could have selected Capresso Espresso Machines as my theme, but it would have been so much harder to write one hundred and fifty pages of content about just Capresso.

Sure, you can do it…and it would be fine. But it gets boring.

I like to keep my themes broader.

But really, it's just a matter of personal preference and style. You'll be ok either way.

Breaking apart your website

Once you have your main theme, the next thing to do is to break apart the structure of your site by category.

I like to do this by focusing on the top 20-30 brands within your theme. With my espressoshack.com website, the themes I chose were:

Espresso Machines
Espresso Accessories
Espresso Beans
Bodum Press
Bosch Espresso
Breville Espresso
Briel
Capresso Coffee
Cuisinart Espresso
DeLonghi
FrancisFrancis
Gaggia
Illy
Jura Capresso
Keurig vs
Krups Espresso
Lavazza
Nespresso
Rancilio
Saeco
Starbucks
Tassimo

Take a good look at that list. The first three categories are simply relevant categories related to espresso machines. The rest are brand names.
But look at the brand names. Some are names, and some are names with the word "Espresso" after them.

For instance, I used "Breville Espresso" as a category, but I could have easily used just "Breville".

Why?

This is where keyword research does come into play a little bit.

You should head over to the free Google Keyword tool (just go to google and search for Google Keyword tool) and type in every one of your main category keywords.

The tool will show you search volume for each word.

In my example, Breville Espresso gets searched for 9,900 times per month at Google, while Breville gets searched for 246,000 times.

Why did I pick the term that gets searched for MUCH less than the other?

Three reasons:

1. It will be much easier to rank for the lower searched-for term.

2. Breville on its own is probably just a little too broad. They make other things besides espresso machines and I want to make sure to only target espresso machines.

3. If I created a web site dedicated to Breville Espresso, I'm also going to pick up a little traffic from people searching for just Breville.

So doing a little research in this area is something worth taking the time to do. And really, it shouldn't take you more than an hour or less to research 20-30 keywords using the Google keyword tool.

How to pick the brands to start with?

So how did I come up with that list of terms to be my main site categories?

I went to Amazon and searched for Espresso Machines. Amazon has a nice feature where they will list brands for you to browse.

Try it out. Go to Amazon.com and type in Espresso Machines.

This is what you'll see:

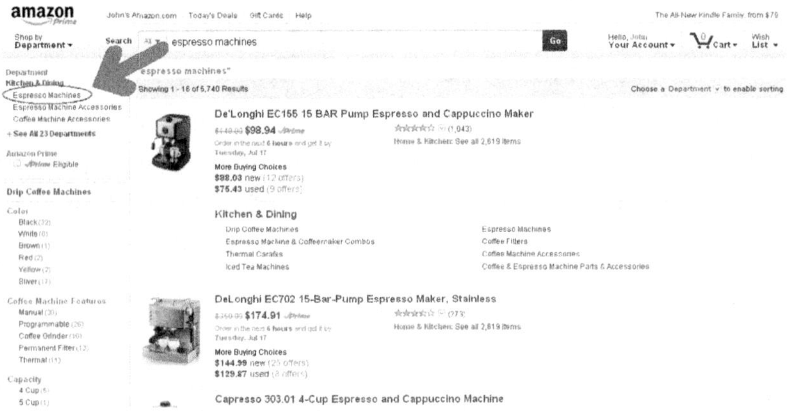

Notice the left-hand side of the screen there's a few choices, namely; espresso machines, espresso machine accessories, and coffee machine accessories.

Click on Espresso machines and this is what you'll see:

Right there on the right hand side is a nice little menu of brands, as well as the number of items Amazon carries in that brand (which is PRICELESS information!).

You'll also see a "Features" menu directly above the Brand menu. That will give you other good ideas of some other categories you might want to create on your website.

In this case, it showed these features:
Steel (296)
Cappuccino (229)
Water Tank (186)
15 Bar (150)
Grinder (130)

Beans (119)
Commercial (100)

That number next to each word is the number of items Amazon is selling that has those features. Again, this is great intel for you to use when determining how to categorize your website.

So let's get back to looking at brands. Go ahead and click on the "See More" link directly under the brand menu and Amazon will show you a huge menu of brands for you to pick from. The page that comes up looks like this:

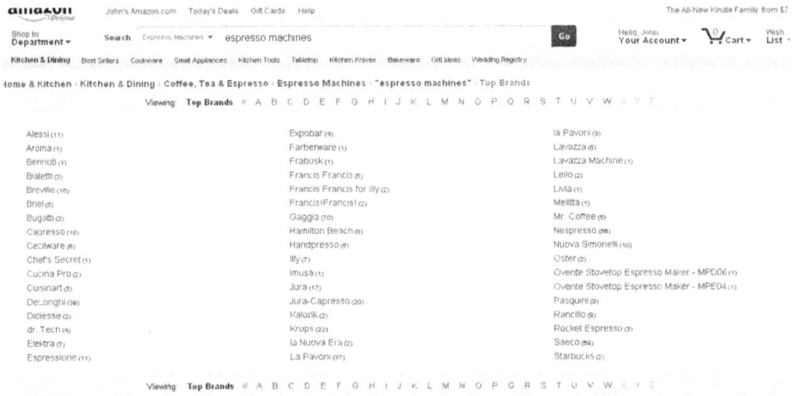

Let's take a closer look at that list…

Alessi (11)
Aroma (1)
Bennoti (1)
Bialetti (3)
Breville (16)
Briel (5)
Bugatti (2)
Capresso (18)
Cecilware (6)
Chef's Secret (1)
Cucina Pro (2)
Cuisinart (5)
DeLonghi (39)
Didiesse (3)
dr. Tech (4)
Elektra (7)
Espressione (11)
Expobar (4)
Farberware (1)
Frabosk (1)
Francis Francis (5)
Francis Francis illy (2)
Francis!Francis! (2)
Gaggia (70)
Hamilton Beach (8)
Handpresso (5)
Illy (7)
Imusa (1)
Jura (17)

Jura-Capresso (20)
Kalorik (2)
Krups (22)
la Nuova Era (2)
La Pavoni (37)
la Pavoni (3)
Lavazza (6)
Lavazza Machine (1)
Lello (2)
Livia (1)
Melitta (1)
Mr. Coffee (5)
Nespresso (56)
Nuova Simonelli (10)
Oster (2)
Ovente Stovetop Espresso Maker - MPD06 (1)
Ovente Stovetop Espresso Maker - MPE04 (1)
Pasquini (9)
Rancilio (9)
Rocket Espresso (3)
Saeco (59)
Starbucks (2)

We're looking at over 50 different brands. That's a good thing because it tells me that there're lots of brands and therefore lots of stuff to write about.

Some niches only have a few brands. You probably want to stay away from any niche that doesn't have a healthy number of brands behind it.

50 is good, but we want to narrow it down. Sure you could write about all of them if you wanted to, but that would create a much larger website and take more time.

I prefer to pick the top 20-30 and write about them, and then if my thick site takes off and Google likes it, I might go back and write about the others.

Narrowing down the list…

So how do you narrow down the list? Two ways.

The first is to simply eyeball it. In our list above, Ovente Stovetop Espresso Maker - MPD06 (1) and Ovente Stovetop Espresso Maker - MPE04 (1) seem odd. I'd dismiss them immediately (or simply choose Ovente as a category).

There will always be oddities in the list like that.

Plus if you're familiar with the brands, you'll know who the important ones are already.

You can also eyeball the count data that Amazon lists right there. See the number between the brackets ( ) next to each word?

That tells you how many items Amazon sells for each brand. Look at "Chef's Secret". It has one item for sale and a generic sounding name. I'd lose that brand immediately.

Generally I like to pick the 20-30 brands with the highest number of items selling at Amazon (but not always).

The more items selling, the more listings you can show on your website and the more people will buy. Plus you know if Amazon is selling a bunch of items from a particular brand, then that brand is popular.

I said two ways of determining…

The other way to pick your categories from that list at Amazon, if you aren't familiar with the brands and can't eyeball it, is to simply run each brand name through the free Google keyword tool.

Look at the traffic data for each keyword and then just pick the best ones.

I like to use Amazon to find my brands because I use an **Amazon widget** to show affiliate products on my site, but you can use anything to get your own data.

There are lots of other shopping sites out there that show lists of brands. Use any of them. It doesn't matter where you get brand names, just be sure to get them some where.

Next Pick Your Page Topics…

Once you've come up with a list of 20-30 brand names or features to use as the main categories of your website, the only thing left to do in this department is determine what you're going to write about in each category.

Again, Amazon is great for this….

Head back to that brand page we just looked at. All the brands are clickable. So go ahead and click on one at Amazon.com

Let's take Capresso, for instance. When I click on it at Amazon.com, I get this page:

The first two listings are:

-Capresso 303.01 4-Cup Espresso and Cappuccino Machine

-Capresso EC100 Pump Espresso and Cappuccino Machine

The other two are Jura-Capresso and I created a whole category of Jura so we'll ignore them.

But let's look at those first two. I wrote about the first one but not the second one...but only because that second one wasn't out yet when I built my site.

If it was, I would have added it to my site.

I think I got the other few Capresso keywords from the Google keyword tool.

Basically, what you're looking for is the most popular items in that category. Pick 3-5 of them and write a one page article for each one.

Do that for each of your 20-30 categories and you've got your website.

It's really as simple as that.

I really like to create a roadmap before I start building my sites. I just use notepad or Microsoft Word to create a list of my 20-30 categories, and beneath each category I write the 3-5 products that I'm going to write about.

So using my espressoshack.com site as an example, my list would look like:

Espresso Machines

- Espresso Machines - The Ultimate Guide
- Espresso Machine Price Guide
- The 3 Best Espresso Machines For Someone Just Starting Out
- Automatic Espresso Machines
- Manual vs. Automatic Espresso Machines - Which Is Best For You?
- How To Buy Your First Espresso Machine

Espresso Accessories

- Espresso Accessories and Replacement Parts
- Baratza Virtuoso Coffee Grinder
- How Important Is The Steam Wand?
- Burr Grinders For Espresso - The Beginners Guide
- How To Find Replacement Parts For Your Espresso Machine
- Coffee Bean Grinders

Espresso Beans

- Espresso Beans - How To Choose The Right Ones
- Espresso Bean Suggestion Guide

- How To Grind Your Coffee Beans For Espresso Or French Press
- French Roast vs. Italian Roast - Which Is Best For Espresso?
- Arabica Beans vs. Robusta Beans - Which Is Best For Espresso?
- Coffee Beans vs. Pods vs. Capsules vs. T-Discs - Which Is Best?

Bodum Press

- Bodum Espresso Machines?
- Bodum New Kenya 34-Ounce Coffee Press
- Bodum 1548-01US Brazil 8-Cup 34-Ounce Coffee Press
- Bodum 1308-16 Columbia 8-Cup Stainless-Steel Thermal Press Pot
- Bodum Young French Press
- How To Buy The Best Bodum French Press

Bosch Espresso

- Bosch Espresso Machines
- Bosch Benvenuto B20 Automatic Espresso Machine
- Bosch Traditional Espresso Machine Or New Coffee Center?
- Bosch Benvenuto B30 Automatic Espresso Machine

- Bosch TCA4101UC Barino Pump Espresso Machine

Breville Espresso

- How Much Should You Spend On A Breville Espresso Machine?
- Breville Barista Express BES860XL Machine with Grinder
- Breville 800ESXL Commercial Triple-Priming Die-Cast Espresso Machine
- Breville ESP8XL cafe Roma Stainless Espresso Maker
- Breville ESP6SXL Cafe Modena
- Breville Espresso Machines

Briel

- Briel Espresso Machines
- Briel Chamonix vs Cuisinart EM-100 Espresso Machine Which Is Best
- Briel ES150PG-TB Space Saver Multi-Pro One Group Espresso Machine
- Briel ES200APG Multi-Pro Stainless Pump Espresso With Auto Espresso Flow
- Briel ES62AF L'Expresso Automatic Cadiz Espresso Machine
- Briel ES35AF Chamonix Pump Espresso Machine

Capresso Coffee

- Capresso Replacement Parts
- Capresso Infinity Conical Burr Grinder
- Capresso 121.01 Ultima Espresso Machine
- Capresso 303.01 4-Cup Espresso And Cappuccino Machine
- Capresso 115.01 Capresso Cafe Espresso Machine

- Capresso Espresso Machines

Cuisinart Espresso

- Cuisinart Espresso Machines
- Cuisinart SS-700 Single-Serve Brewing System
- Cuisinart CBM-18 Programmable Conical Burr Mill
- Cuisinart EM-200 Espresso Maker
- Cuisinart EM-100 Espresso Machine

DeLonghi

- DeLonghi Espresso Machines
- DeLonghi BAR32 Retro Pump-Driven 35-ounce Espresso Maker
- DeLonghi EC155 Espresso Maker
- DeLonghi EC702 15-Bar Pump Espresso Maker

- Delonghi EC270 Espresso Machine

FrancisFrancis

- FrancisFrancis! Espresso Machines
- FrancisFrancis! X6 Trio Espresso Machine
- FrancisFrancis! 208003 X8 iperEspresso Machine
- FrancisFrancis! X1 Ground Espresso Machine
- FrancisFrancis! X7 iperEspresso Machine

Gaggia

- Gaggia Espresso Machines
- Gaggia 12300 Baby Class Manual Espresso Machine
- Gaggia 90951 Platinum Vision Automatic Espresso Machine
- Gaggia 14101 Classic Espresso Machine
- Gaggia 16100 Evolution Home Espresso Cappuccino Machine

Illy

- Illy Espresso and Coffee Beans
- Illy Coffee Pods

- Illy Coffee Capsules
- Are Illy Beans Good For Making Espresso?
- How To Pick The Illy Coffee Bean Thats Right For You

Jura Capresso

- Jura-Capresso Espresso Machines
- Jura-Capresso Impressa J5 Automatic Coffee and Espresso Center
- Jura-Capresso ENA5 Automatic Coffee and Espresso Center
- Jura-Capresso 13422 Impressa C9 Automatic Espresso Center
- Jura Capresso 13185 Impressa F7 Espresso Machine

Keurig vs

- Keurig Espresso Machines and K-Cups
- Keurig B-70 Platinum Single-Cup Home Brewing System
- Keurig B-60 Gourmet Single-Cup Home-Brewing System
- Keurig B-40 Elite Gourmet Single-Cup Home Brewing System

- How To Store Your Keurig K-Cups

Krups Espresso

- Krups Espresso Machines
- Should Your First Espresso Machine Be A Krups?
- Krups XP1020 750-Watt Steam Espresso Machine
- Krups XP5240 Precise Tamp Pump Espresso Machine
- Krups XP5220 Precise Tamp Pump Espresso Machine

Lavazza

- Lavazza Espresso Machines
- Lavazza Blue LB2210 Single-Serve Espresso Machine
- Lavazza Point Ep850 Aroma Point Espresso Machine
- Lavazza Point One-Cup Espresso Beverage System

Nespresso

- Nespresso Espresso Machines
- Nespresso D290 Concept Espresso and Coffeemaker
- Nespresso D90-S1 Essenza Single-Serve Manual Espresso Machine
- Nespresso CitiZ Automatic Espresso Maker
- Nespresso C100 Espresso Machine

Rancilio

- Rancilio Espresso Machines
- Is A Rancilio Espresso Machine Right For You?
- Rancilio Rocky Burr Grinder with Doser
- Rancilio ST-1 Epoca Semi-Automatic Espresso Machine
- Rancilio Silvia Espresso Machine

Saeco

- Saeco Espresso Machines
- Saeco Espresso Machines Vs. Gaggia Espresso Machines - Which Should You Choose?
- Saeco 4038 Vienna Plus 15-Bar Pump Super-Automatic Espresso Machine
- Saeco Odea Giro Super-Automatic Espresso Machine

- Saeco 30013 Aroma Traditional Espresso Machine

Starbucks

- Starbucks Espresso Machines and Beans
- Starbucks Accessories - Too Expensive?
- Starbucks vs. Illy - Which Beans Make Better Espresso?
- Starbucks Sirena Espresso Machine

Tassimo

- Tassimo Espresso Machines
- Tassimo Brewbot vs. Nespresso Single Cup - Which Is Better?
- Tassimo Hot Beverage System
- Tassimo Single Serve Coffee Brewer
- Tassimo T20 Single Serve Coffee Brewer

You'll notice that some of them are simply the product name, while some of them are more narrative in nature.

That's something you just want to eyeball. Using the Google keyword tool will help you in that area. For instance, I picked the keyword:

"How Much Should You Spend On A Breville Espresso Machine?"

…simply because a lot of the Breville products are similar and I didn't want to keep writing the same reviews over and over again.

Narrative articles like that are important and you should try to sprinkle them throughout your thick site in all the categories if possible. Make them seem like "buying guides", people love those.

Look Over That List…

Check out the some of the things I did, especially the "Vs" articles. It might seem weird to cross pollinate products in categories, ie talking about Gaggia machines in the Saeco section like I did in this article:

"Saeco Espresso Machines Vs. Gaggia Espresso Machines Which Should You Choose?"

But "vs" articles where you compare and contrast two different machines across brands are VERY good at pulling in search engine traffic.

I'd go so far as to suggest that they were some of my most popular articles across the entire website. I stumbled on them quite by accident but they've turned out to be great traffic generators. Give them a try!

In Conclusion…

The whole concept is fairly simple and straight forward. You can really just break it down into three simple steps:

1. Pick a broad theme for your thick site based on a type of product of some sort.

2. Break up the site into 20-30 categories based on brand names or broad features within the theme.

3. Write 5-6 pages per category about the most popular product of that brand, sprinkling in a how-to article of some sort for each category if appropriate.

In the next chapter I'll talk about the content for your thick site. Believe me when I say that it's all about content. Even though Google may be wishy-washy these days; one thing hasn't changed....content is still king.

CHAPTER THREE
Thick Site Content Creation

Now that you've picked out the main theme for your site as well as your categories and created a list of article names to write about, the next thing to do is write the actual content.

Actually, I might have talked about actually building the site first, because you can't add content pages until you've created the actual website.

But I figured writing content goes along with picking your site theme and categories so I thought I'd talk about it now instead of later.

Content!

Yes content. It's the single most important step in any thick site strategy.

Without content, you have nothing. And not just any content, you need unique content.

Don't try to use reprinted articles from elsewhere, and don't try to spin private label rights articles either.

Those strategies can work well for thin sites, but not for thick ones.

The entire point of a thick site is to generate traffic from the search engines, and you simply can't do that over the long run without unique content.

So What Should You Write About?

It's really pretty straight forward.

Each page of your website should focus on one item, or in most cases, one product.

Sticking with our espressoshack.com example, here's a list of pages I wrote for the Capresso section of the site that I've already shown you before:

- Capresso Replacement Parts
- Capresso Infinity Conical Burr Grinder
- Capresso 121.01 Ultima Espresso Machine
- Capresso 303.01 4-Cup Espresso And Cappuccino Machine

- Capresso 115.01 Capresso Cafe Espresso Machine
- Capresso Espresso Machines

Each of those is one page, and on each of those pages you'll find a 500-1200 word article about whatever it's targeting.

Each of those is also the title of the page and that page's main keyword phrase.

I like to treat each page as a product review. Pretend you're trying to convince a person to buy that product (in essence, you ARE trying to do that because at the bottom of each page you'll put a link to amazon.com where they can buy it!).

Be persuasive, but more importantly; be informative.

This is where you'll have to do a little research on each item. I like to use Amazon.com for research because they always have a nice synopsis of the product, a list of its main features, and lots of reviews from past customers.

Use ALL that information, but re-write it in your own words as if you were talking about it yourself to a friend.

Sometimes Amazon isn't enough…

Sometimes they won't have a very good write-up about the product, or won't list the features, or won't have any reviews.

When that happens, I tend to go straight to the company website and read what they have to say about the product. Or sometimes I'll head over to Google and search other shopping sites for info.

It really doesn't matter where you get your information; the important thing is to write as much as you can.

Don't just talk about the features of the products, describe the problems that it solves.

An espresso machine that has an auto grinder and auto disposal feature is nice, but explain how it will make a person's life easier.

Paint a picture for them in their mind. Why will this product make their life better?

It's about selling, not describing. There's tons of sites out there that just regurgitate features. If you do the same thing you'll never stand out and get free Google traffic.

Customer Reviews

I always like to summarize the Amazon reviews. Are most of them good? Are some of them bad? What did the bad reviews talk about?

Sometimes talking about the bad things is a good way to dismiss hesitation in people.

Create a mathematical sketchup of the reviews…

"219 people gave it a four star review and 43 gave it a two star..that's an average of…blah blah blah and I think that means that blah blah blah…"

You get the idea. Add perspective, don't regurgitate.

Buying Guides…

Don't just talk about specific products. In each of your categories, you should try to write some sort of buying guide for that category.

Some of the buying guide type articles I wrote for espressoshack.com were:

- Espresso Machine Price Guide
- The 3 Best Espresso Machines For Someone Just Starting Out
- Automatic Espresso Machines
- Manual vs. Automatic Espresso Machines - Which Is Best For You?
- How To Buy Your First Espresso Machine
- How Important Is The Steam Wand
- Burr Grinders For Espresso - The Beginners Guide

- How To Find Replacement Parts For Your Espresso Machine
- Espresso Bean Suggestion Guide
- How To Grind Your Coffee Beans For Espresso Or French Press
- How To Buy The Best Bodum French Press
- How Much Should You Spend On A Breville Espresso Machine?
- Tassimo Brewbot vs. Nespresso Single Cup - Which Is Better?
- How To Pick The Illy Coffee Bean That's Right For You
- How To Store Your Keurig K-Cups
- Should Your First Espresso Machine Be A Krups?
- Is A Rancilio Espresso Machine Right For You?
- Starbucks Accessories - Too Expensive?

Take a minute to really look through that list. You'll see several themes going on.

- How To Buy
- How To Use
- How To Fix
- How Much To Spend
- Buying Your First X
- Taking Care of X (storing, getting accessories, etc)
- Vs

I especially like the "vs." articles. You can pick two of any of your products and write a simple article comparing and contrasting them; then give your opinion on which is better.

It's interesting for your readers, and Google really eats that kind of thing up. The "vs." articles on my espressoshack.com site were some of the most viewed.

People love them.

And it's infinite…you can always compare and contrast two different things. There's no end of content possibilities there.

Creating Authority

Some people refer to thick sites as "Authority Sites" and I think after reading that list of articles you might be able to tell why.

It's because you're essentially putting yourself out there as an authority and using that authority to help people make a buying decision.

It doesn't matter if you aren't really an authority. Believe me, by the time you finish building your website…you WILL be an authority of sorts.

Why? Because you'll have to do a lot of research to write those articles, and in the course of that research you'll become an authority.

You'll learn the stuff. And that's all an authority really is.

But there's More…

Authority doesn't just mean that you know what you're talking about; it's also a technical term that Google uses.

You see, when Google decides that you're site is an "Authority" it starts to treat it differently in the Search Engine Results.

Let's take my MarketingFool.com website for instance. It's become one of the leading websites on the Internet about Adsense marketing.

Not only that, but we've grown into a huge community. Lot's of people interact with the site, share the articles I write on facebook and twitter, and post comments etc.

Google has come to realize how important my website is to the Adsense community and has determined that it's an "Authority" on the subject.

So they treat the site differently in the search engine results, check it out:

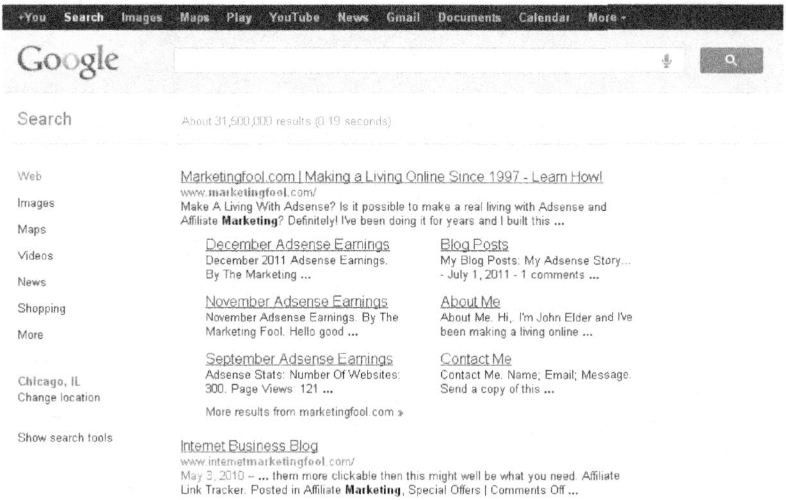

See how it lists the different pages of my site, sort of indented below the main listing? Not to mention ranking 1st.

That's what happens when your site becomes an "Authority" in Google's eye.

Everyone else's listing just looks like this:

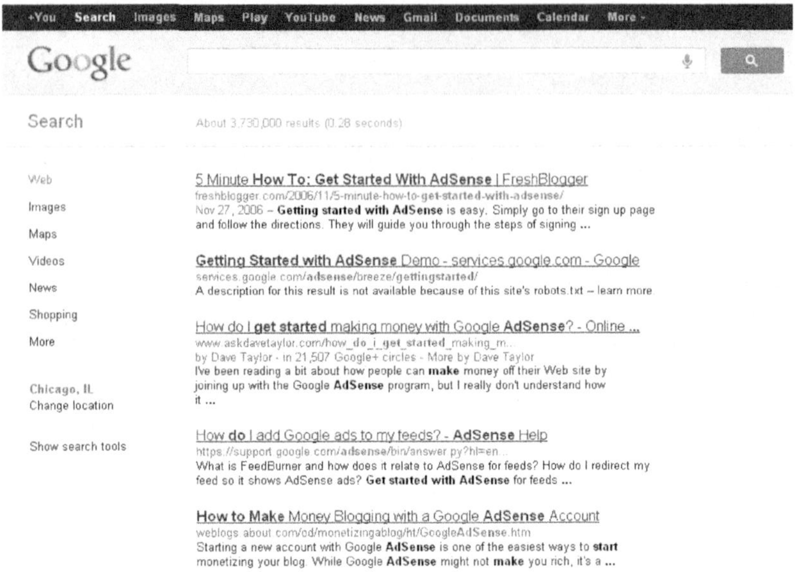

See the difference? You can imagine what an impact that will have on your search traffic can't you?

Anyone searching for a term who see's a listing like mine is going to be much more likely to click on it than the other

ones, simply because that listing takes up so much real estate and draws the eye right to it.

That's really the goal of any thick site, right there; to become an authority in Google's search results.

I'll talk more about ranking your thick sites in a later chapter.

Category Pages...

I almost forgot to mention category pages, though I did brush on them briefly when I talked about the overall strategy earlier in the book.

Each category should have a page of content itself. Since most of your categories are going to be brands, you should write about the brand for that category page.

For instance, Capresso Coffee was a category of my espressoshack.com website.

So for that page I talked about the Capresso Company, gave their mailing address and website information, talked about how you can contact them for support reasons, etc.

Check it out here:
http://espressoshack.marketingfool.com/capresso.html

I also talked a little bit about the history of the company. You can't always do that and make it interesting, but with espresso machines you can because a lot of the time the company itself has a sort of romantic history.

Plus it's good to say that a company has been in business for 20 years making these things and that you can depend on them, or on the other hand, explaining that the company is very new and giving your readers a heads up to keep their eyes open until that company has proven itself.

It's really very easy to knock out those types of pages. Most of the time I go straight to the company website for info. Almost all major corporations have a section of their website dedicated to telling their story and giving a little history.

Most of the time they do your work for you, you just have to re-write it all in your own words.

Think of the category page as a doorway page to the rest of the pages in that category. Give some background info, contact info, any interesting facts about the company, where they're located etc.

It's pretty straight forward.

You can see all my category pages by clicking on the links on the right hand menu on any page at the site, those pages are:

http://espressoshack.marketingfool.com/espresso-machines.html

http://espressoshack.marketingfool.com/espresso-accessories.html

http://espressoshack.marketingfool.com/espresso-beans.html

http://espressoshack.marketingfool.com/bodum.html

http://espressoshack.marketingfool.com/bosch.html

http://espressoshack.marketingfool.com/breville.html

http://espressoshack.marketingfool.com/briel.html

http://espressoshack.marketingfool.com/capresso.html

http://espressoshack.marketingfool.com/cuisinart.html

http://espressoshack.marketingfool.com/delonghi.html

http://espressoshack.marketingfool.com/francisfrancis.html

http://espressoshack.marketingfool.com/gaggia.html

http://espressoshack.marketingfool.com/illy.html

http://espressoshack.marketingfool.com/jura-capresso.html

http://espressoshack.marketingfool.com/keurig.html

http://espressoshack.marketingfool.com/krups.html

http://espressoshack.marketingfool.com/lavazza.html

http://espressoshack.marketingfool.com/nespresso.html

http://espressoshack.marketingfool.com/rancilio.html

http://espressoshack.marketingfool.com/saeco.html

http://espressoshack.marketingfool.com/starbucks.html

http://espressoshack.marketingfool.com/tassimo.html

To Write Content Yourself - Or Hire Someone?

Writing is hard work…believe me I know! There's nothing wrong with hiring other people to write your content for you as long as you explain to them all the thing's I've discussed in this book.

The problem is, any decent writer is going to charge you anywhere from $5 an article up to $50 or even more depending on how much research you want them to do and how specific you want the article to become.

If you're going to put up 150 articles, at $5 each that would cost you $750 for some very low quality articles and could even run you as much as $7,500 for high quality stuff; and anywhere in between.

My espressoshack.com website only brought in around $3,200 dollars. You could easily spend that much buying content, leaving a whole lot of risk and very little reward.

It's always a good idea to start out writing your own content. As you get better at building these types of websites, you might farm out some of the writing work.

But I don't suggest you do that at first.

One Alternative…

There's lots of software and services out there that promise unique content cheaply, but most of them don't work very well or are outright frauds (packaging up previously used private label rights work and spinning them and trying to fool people).

But there is one piece of software that's really good at creating unique content and costs just pennies a day to use as often as you want.

It's a good resource to use for someone just starting out who doesn't want to write his/her own content but can't afford to hire a writer.

It's called **Article Builder** you can find it at: (**http://www.marketingfool.com/articlebuilderrocks.html**)

That tool was created by Jonathan Leger, one of the pioneers of Internet marketing software. He's the guy that created the words leading spinner software, aptly called **The Best Spinner**.

I've used the Best Spinner for years and I highly recommend it, just like I highly recommend his Article Builder software.

He only ever sells 1,000 licenses at any time for the software, and that's a great thing. Why? Because any software can only create so much content.

If hundreds of thousands of people used it, the quality of the articles would plummet. By capping the number at 1,000 users, Jonathan makes sure that it keeps spitting out quality work.

That means you may or may not be able to buy the thing. It comes as a yearly subscription, so as people's subscriptions expire spots do open up.

I suggest you check out the website for it, listed above and take advantage if you're lucky enough to grab a spot. You won't be disappointed.

CHAPTER FOUR

Webhosting Your Thick Site

To put a website online, you need to purchase webhosting. You also need to register a domain name for your site. Let's start there...

Picking A Domain Name...

At MarketingFool.com I talk a LOT about thin sites and using .info domains because they're really cheap and work just as well as .com's.

But that's only true when it comes to Thin Adsense sites. Thin sites entail a whole different strategy than Thick sites.

When it comes to thick websites, you really need to purchase a .com domain.

Why? Because we're building a branded website. You want it to stick in people's minds. It should be something catchy that they can remember.

Like EspressoShack.com That's a great example.

The best thing to do is use your main keyword alone. If espressoMachines.com was available I would have taken it in a second!

We call that an Exact Match Domain (EMD).

But today, it's going to be VERY rare to find an exact match domain that isn't already taken. So you have to be creative.

I like to keep a list of short words in mind to tack onto the end of an EMD. Think of things like:

- Shop
- Pro
- Reviews
- Store
- Hut
- Shack
- Discount
- Sale
- Now
- Here

You get the idea. You want to tack those words onto the END of your domain, not the beginning. For instance, some examples using my espresso theme and those words above would be:

- EspressoShop.com
- EspressoPro.com
- EspressoReviews.com
- EspressoStore.com
- EspressoHut.com
- EspressoShack.com
- EspressoDiscount.com
- EspressoSale.com
- EspressoNow.com
- EspressoHere.com

You get the idea.

Try to keep it as short as possible, and as snappy as possible. That list is by no means exhaustive. Just about any short word you can think of will work. Be creative!

The trick is to find one that hasn't already been taken.

What about .net and .org?

Stay away from them. Sometimes they work ok, but it's harder to sell a site that doesn't have a .com address. It's a strike against you. (You may get a lower selling price!)

People like and are used to .com addresses so stick with them.

Where to register your domain name?

There are lots of reputable domain registration companies out there but I like to stick with **Godaddy**.

If you use this URL:
(**http://www.marketingfool.com/godaddyrocks.html**)

They'll give you a special offer on your domain. You'll pay just $7.99 versus the $10-11 you'd normally pay there or elsewhere.

Take advantage of that deal soon because I don't know how much longer it will last.

Even without that deal, Godaddy is an industry leader in Domain Name Registration. It's always important to stick with the big names for something like this.

If you're doing thin sites and buying domain names in bulk, Godaddy often offers amazing bulk discounts. You can read my blog at MarketingFool.com to learn more about that sort of thing.

But even if you plan on just building a few or a few dozen thick websites, Godaddy won't steer you wrong.

Webhosting Your Site…

Domain names are important, but hosting your site is even more important.

Choosing a professional web host is incredibly important. There's a ton of different things that can go wrong, from misconfigured servers to hackers taking down your site.

You want a web hosting provider that you can count on. I've tried dozens over the years and I can boil it down to just a couple that I trust.

I suggest either:

- **Hostgator (http://www.marketingfool.com/hostgatorrocks.html)**

- **Servint (http://www.marketingfool.com/servintrocks.html)**

What's the difference? It depends…

Hostgator

Hostgator is really one of the leading webhosting companies in the world. They really focus on people that don't have a lot of programming knowledge.

That is to say, you don't really need to know anything about web server technology to use Hostgator.

Ease of use is the name of the game with Hostgator. The tradeoff is that there servers aren't heavy duty. But that might be ok if you just plan on creating a few websites (say 5-50).

I recommend you purchase their Aluminum Reseller Package (click the "Reseller Hosting" link at the top of their website).

It allows you to host as many websites as you want (within reason) for one low monthly price of about $25/mo.

If you need more space or bandwidth, you can easily upgrade to their larger packages. Their copper package costs around $35 and their biggest package, the Diamond package runs around $99 a month.

The only reason to upgrade is if you need more space or bandwidth (ie your sites grow very large or get lots of traffic).

The $25 aluminum package is perfect for someone starting out.

And hostgator has tons of tutorials, videos, and support to teach you how to get up and running. It's really just a matter of pointing and clicking a few things and then logging into your wordpress admin area, dropping in your Clickbump wordpress themes, then writing content.

Servint

On the other hand, I recommend Servint for power users who need serious hardware and bandwidth.

For instance, if you're doing a batch of several hundred or thousand thin sites, Servint has the power you need.

I suggest you start out with their Essential VPS package and upgrade throughout the VPS packages as you grow.

Eventually you may need to upgrade to their dedicated server packages, and they can handle the upgrades themselves.

I really like Servint for their professional support and their solid hardware and hosting packages.

Why is web hosting so important?

I recently wrote an article about this very thing for MarketingFool.com, I thought it would be appropriate for me to reprint it here:

Adsense WebHosting Disasters
By: John Elder – The Marketing Fool!

Today I want to talk about Webhosting and how incredibly important it is to building an Adsense Empire.

Most people don't put a lot of thought into Webhosting. Most of the people I talk to simply go with a cheap host like Hostgator.

That's fine for someone just starting out, but if you've got very large thick sites that get a lot of traffic, or a network of hundreds or thousands of thin sites; you need a more professional webhost.

I use Servint and really like them, for one reason…

Their support is quick and professional…and downright amazing.

Let Me Tell you What Happened To Me…

Last week I added close to a thousand new websites to one of my accounts at servint. These were all thin sites, hand coded with php and html (not wordpress).

They didn't take up much space or nearly the amount of resources that a wordpress site would take up (wordpress is a massive resource hog). But even so, the amount of traffic that the new sites started to generate quickly crashed my server.

I couldn't even log in to restart apache (the web server). I was completely frozen out.

I pointed my browser towards the Servint tech support website and submitted a tech support ticket. Within 5 minutes or so the tech support guy had restarted apache and fixed the problem.

He then analyzed my account and realized that I was way over booked with sites for the hosting package I was currently on.

After talking about it for a few minutes I agreed to upgrade my account to one that we determined would handle the load better.

Guess how much of a hassle the upgrade was… go ahead and guess.

None, it was no hassle at all. Within minutes the tech guy had done everything for me.

That's amazing. And It Doesn't Stop There…

Last week on another of my websites that's hosted on a different account (also at Servint) I wrote a blog post that was quickly picked up by social media sites. Traffic spiked out of control as several thousand people pounced on the site in seconds to read the article.

The server crashed.

I did the same thing again, pointed my browser toward the servint tech support website and submitted a ticket. Within 2 or 3 minutes the tech support guy had upgraded that particular account to a plan that was several pay grades higher in cost – but one that would handle the spike in traffic.

"This is gonna cost me a fortune" I thought to myself.

That's when the tech guy hit me with a broadside. He said "I upgraded your account to the X package to handle the traffic. I put a 7-day timer on it so it will stay at that package for 7-days to handle this spike in traffic, then it will auto adjust itself back to your regular hosting package…

…we'll call it a free trial" he said.

Wow!!! Do you have any idea how amazing that sort of tech support is?

It's Truly Amazing In This Day And Age…

I don't want to be overly-dramatic, but this is our life and livelihoods here. If your server goes down, you don't make money. Try getting that sort of support from any other webhosting company. Just try!

I've been around the block. I've been online since 1996 and I've used a dozen different web hosting providers, but I've never experienced anything that amazing. And that sort of thing happens all the time with Servint for everyone I've ever talked to who uses them.

Heck, with most webhosts I've used in the past; if you submit a support ticket – they may get to you that day, or the next day…sometime. And they don't give out "free trials" when they have you over a barrel.

So take my advice, choose the best when it comes to web hosting. Choose Servint so that you can…

Keep on building!

-John Elder
The Marketing Fool!

I hope that convinces you to use either Servint or Hostgator. Sure there are cheaper alternatives, but I can't tell you how many horror stories I've had personally with shoddy web hosting providers.

And many people I've talked to have echoed that sentiment time and time again. Why mess around?

I'm a big Servint fan, but if you're just starting out; I highly recommend you go with Hostgator (unless you have a technical or programming background).

Servint does have a learning curve. It isn't as intuitive, and there aren't as many point and click type options. You really need to either know what you're doing or at least be technically inclined and able to figure it out.

Hostgator, on the other hand, is purely point and click. Once you order your hosting plan - they'll send you an email telling you exactly how to proceed step by step…

And then it's just a matter of point and click and you're set up and ready to go.

One of the sections of my special **MarketingFool.com Members Only Website** is dedicated to helping our members with their webhosting.

So if this all seems confusing and overwhelming to you, you're not alone! You may want to consider becoming a member and we'll walk you through everything, answer any questions, and even work with you till everything's set up and ready to go. Check it out at:

www.marketingfool.com/member

CHAPTER FIVE
Site Layout and Design

So you've got your domain name and web hosting account. Now it's time to get down to business building the actual website. I talked a little bit about this earlier in the introduction of this book but it's time to expand on it.

First off, should you use wordpress or hand code the site yourself using html and php. Or should you use some other CMS or software to build the site.

The answer is, truly, that it doesn't matter.

I write my sites by hand using HTML and php because I've been doing it for over 15 years and I can write HTML and php in my sleep.

There are lots of benefits to that. First, my sites are tiny and very fast compared to wordpress sites, so I can cram many many more sites on a single web server and pay less in bandwidth charges every month.

But if you don't have any sort of coding experience then you should stick with an out of the box solution like wordpress. If you do use wordpress, there are a number of very good wordpress themes that you can purchase that have proven to work very well as thick site templates.

The one that I recommend (because they sell a template that looks almost exactly like the one I use with my HTML/php sites) is called **Clickbump**.

You can find them here:
(**http://www.marketingfool.com/clickbumprocks.html**)

The basic package that he sells has some good templates that I've used in the past for some of my sites, and he also offers premium templates that you can buy and add on as well.

It's the premium templates that will really blow you away. One of them, xfactored2.0 I think it's called, is nearly the exact template I use myself.

So if you want to run wordpress and you want a template that nearly exactly mirrors mine, I suggest you pick up Scott's Clickbump engine and add on the xFactored2.0 premium template and maybe the "Authority" template.

They aren't very expensive either. I think the base Clickbump engine is like less than $60 and the premium templates are under $10-15 each (and he has a ton of really nice ones to choose from).

After you install them, you don't have to worry about anything else but writing content, and that's as easy as logging into your wordpress admin area and creating a new
post, then typing.

You can head over to espressoshack.marketingfool.com to see how I layout all my thick websites.

It's pretty straight forward.

Basic Site Layout

My thick sites basically have two different page layouts. One for the main homepage, and one for all the rest of the content pages.

The two layouts are very similar, but the homepage is slightly different. Let's look at the homepage layout first. Take a look at it here:

http://espressoshack.marketingfool.com/index.html

You'll see at the very top of the screen, instead of the regular adsense ad that I put on the content pages, there's a quote about espresso.

I like to keep ads off the home page just because that seems to get a little more Google love. If your site ever gets checked by a Google quality reviewer, they WILL penalize you for having ads on the homepage.

Plus I think it looks more professional. And a dirty little secret is that very few people will go to your homepage. Most of your traffic will come from long tail keyword searches pointing to your inner pages.

Directly below that you'll see little pictures and snippets of descriptions for each major category of the site.

The bottom of the homepage:

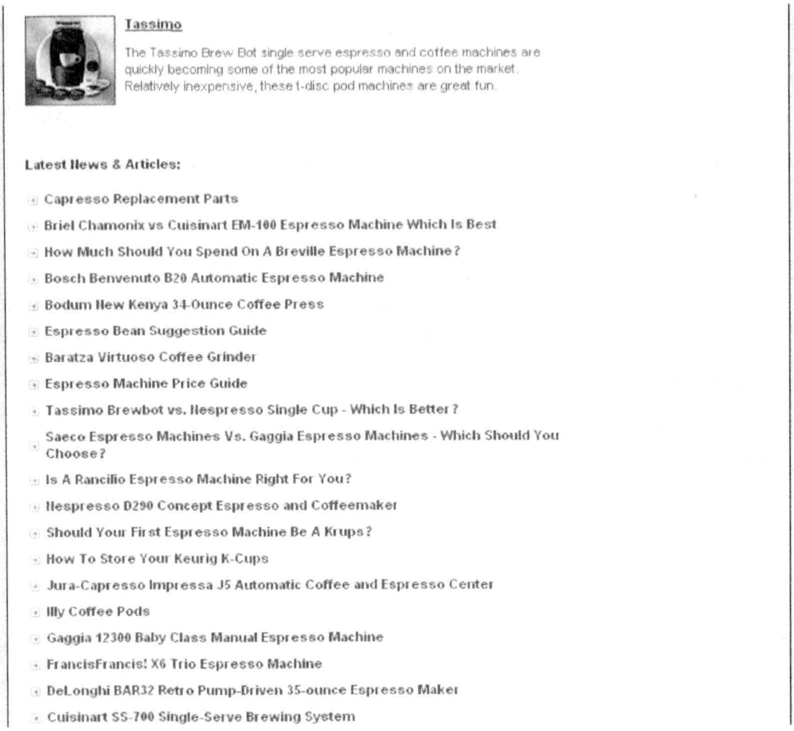

Tassimo

The Tassimo Brew Bot single serve espresso and coffee machines are quickly becoming some of the most popular machines on the market. Relatively inexpensive, these t-disc pod machines are great fun.

Latest News & Articles:

- Capresso Replacement Parts
- Briel Chamonix vs Cuisinart EM-100 Espresso Machine Which Is Best
- How Much Should You Spend On A Breville Espresso Machine?
- Bosch Benvenuto B20 Automatic Espresso Machine
- Bodum New Kenya 34-Ounce Coffee Press
- Espresso Bean Suggestion Guide
- Baratza Virtuoso Coffee Grinder
- Espresso Machine Price Guide
- Tassimo Brewbot vs. Nespresso Single Cup - Which Is Better?
- Saeco Espresso Machines Vs. Gaggia Espresso Machines - Which Should You Choose?
- Is A Rancilio Espresso Machine Right For You?
- Nespresso D290 Concept Espresso and Coffeemaker
- Should Your First Espresso Machine Be A Krups?
- How To Store Your Keurig K-Cups
- Jura-Capresso Impressa J5 Automatic Coffee and Espresso Center
- Illy Coffee Pods
- Gaggia 12300 Baby Class Manual Espresso Machine
- FrancisFrancis! X6 Trio Espresso Machine
- DeLonghi BAR32 Retro Pump-Driven 35-ounce Espresso Maker
- Cuisinart SS-700 Single-Serve Brewing System

Notice at the bottom, below the snippets and pictures is a list of content pages on the site.

I don't like ALL the pages, but I will list 50 or so. I find it helps get all the pages indexed at Google by listing them on the main page, so I'll rotate them from time to time – especially at the beginning when the site is just getting started.

Then at the very bottom of the page I'll put a link to the sitemap page which WILL list all the pages of the site: **http://espressoshack.marketingfool.com/sitemap.html**

Content Pages

So that's the homepage. The rest of the pages of your thick site will be content pages, and they'll all have the same basic layout.

I've discussed this layout already, you can see it on any page of the site, but here's the picture again just so that it's fresh in your memory:

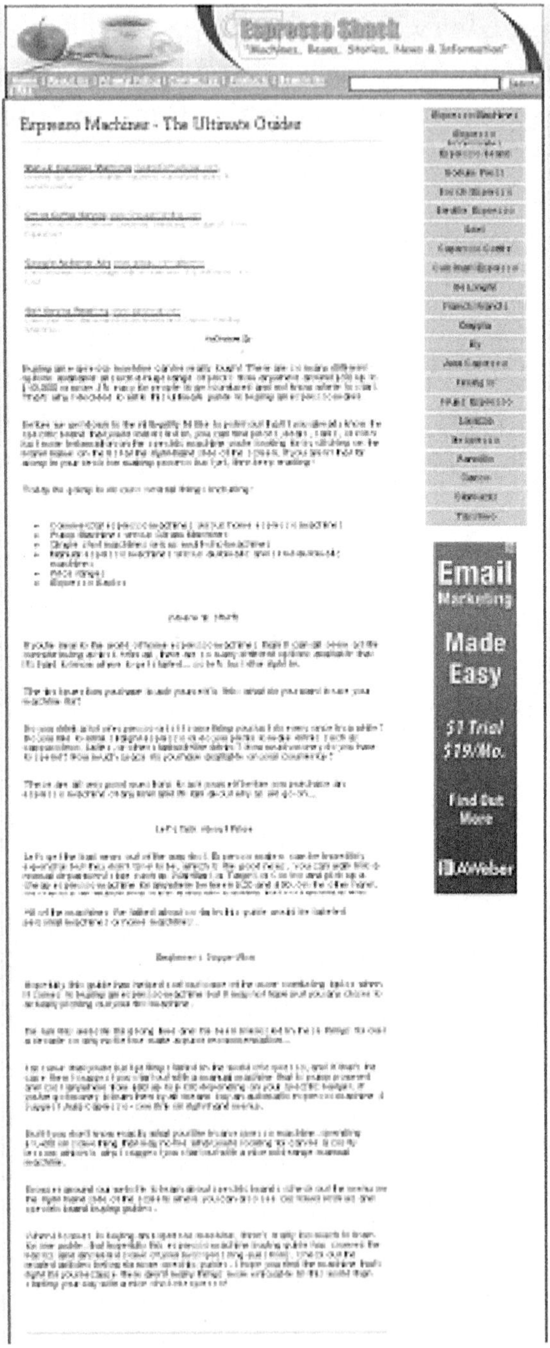
Espresso Shack
"Machines, Beans, Stories, News & Information"
Espresso Machines - The Ultimate Guide
Email
Marketing
Made
Easy
$1 Trial
$19/Mo.
Find Out
More
AWeber

It's pretty straight forward.

- Header at the top
- followed by utility page links directly below
- followed by the main adsense ad block (that I'll talk about next)
- followed by the main content of the page
- followed by an amazon affiliate ad
- followed by links to other pages in that category
- And a menu of all category pages on the right side with a long adsense image ad underneath it.

Adsense Ads

One thing we do really need to talk about is adsense ads. If you take a look at my site, you'll see that I use two different types of ads.

The main adsense ad block that goes at the top of each page is 336 x 280 in size and looks like this:

Tassimo® Official Site www.tassimodirect.com
Take 15% Off Your Order Site Wide! Stock Up On All Your Favorites Now.

Self Service Retailing www.autoretail.com
Own your own Automated Store kiosks and Custom Vending Machines

Office Coffee Machines OfficeCoffee.BuyerZone.com
Compare Prices, Services & Save Find the Best Deal Today!

Which Espresso Machine? www.ConsumerSearch.com
No-bull research and ratings Free unbiased reviews and top picks

AdChoices

I like to use that sized ad for nearly all my sites, both thick and thin. But look at the color scheme because that's important.

First off, there's no border around the ad. That's important because I want it to look more like a menu of links than an ad.

Next you'll notice that the link color is a sort of bright blue. Technically the color is #0000FF and that's what you'll type into the "Title" color section at Google when you create your own ads.

Some people like to use a color that blends into the surrounding website's color scheme more, but not me. I like

the links in my ads to JUMP out and #0000FF bright blue does just that.

Next notice that the text right next to the blue link is a sort of muted dark gray. Technically that color is: #333333 and you should use that for the "URL" color field when building your ads.

Directly under the Link and URL is the ad itself, and I've chosen a light gray color to make that as unobtrusive as possible. The technical color is: #C0C0C0 and you should use that in the "Text" color field at Google.

One last thing to note is text font and size. I use the default font family and the "Small" size option when creating my ads at Google.

I almost forgot…and this is crucial…when you create ads at Google Adsense, they give you the option to create "Text" ads (like the one above), "Image/Rich Media" ads, or "both".

People are always inclined to pick Image/Rich media ads, but in my experience the text ads work best. Also don't chose "both", what you really want is JUST text ads for this spot.

So when you log into Google Adsense and create an adsense ad unit, the final setting should look something like this:

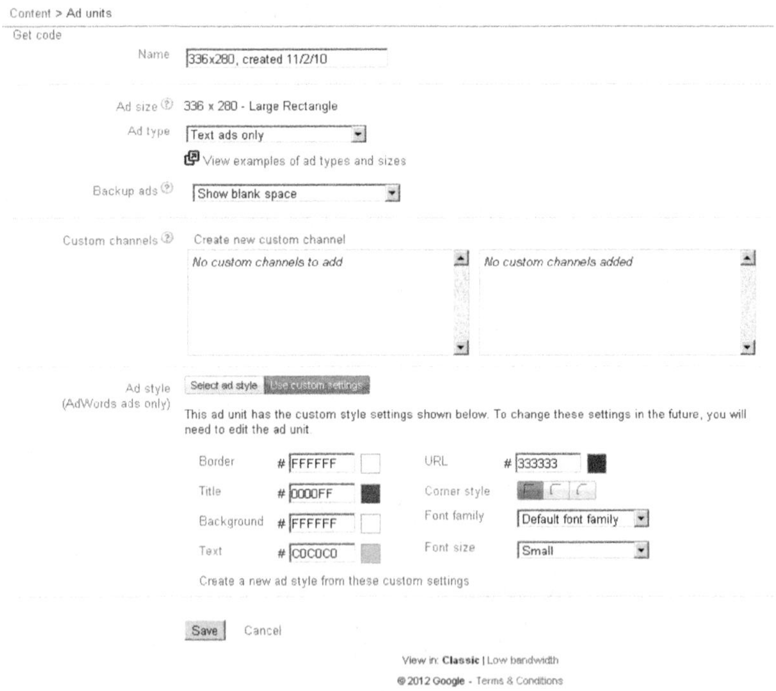

Notice the color selection at the bottom, that's where you enter the color codes I just mentioned.

It's pretty straight forward.

I create one ad block with those parameters and use it on every single page, right at the top of the page directly above the content and below the site header.

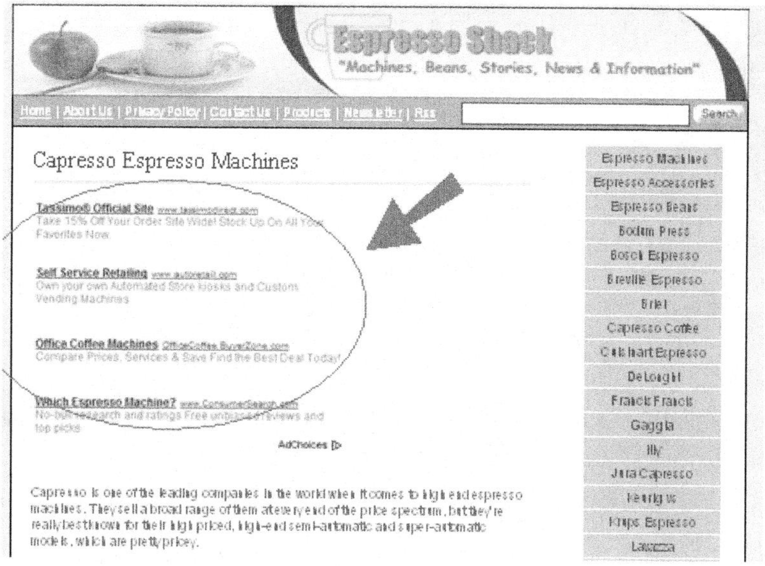

The other ad I use goes directly under the right side menu. For that ad I DO use Image/Rich Media ads. I use the long vertical ads, which are 120 x 600 in size.

I like to use JUST Image/Rich media ads here, but you can use both that and text. It doesn't really matter. Personally I think it makes the site look more professional if it's an image ad.

And it also draws attention away from the main ad block at the top of the page. I don't mean it draws the eye away from the main ad at the top of the page, I mean it camouflages it.

People think the long image ad on the side of the page is the "Ad" and the text links at the top of the page are just "links" that they might find useful.

I'm trying to say that it makes them trust the top ad more, and makes them more likely to click on it because they might not realize they're clicking on an ad.

But that's purely anecdotal, I've not actually tested to see if that's the case…but that's what my gut tells me.

Anyway, here's what the ad on the side of the screen looks like:

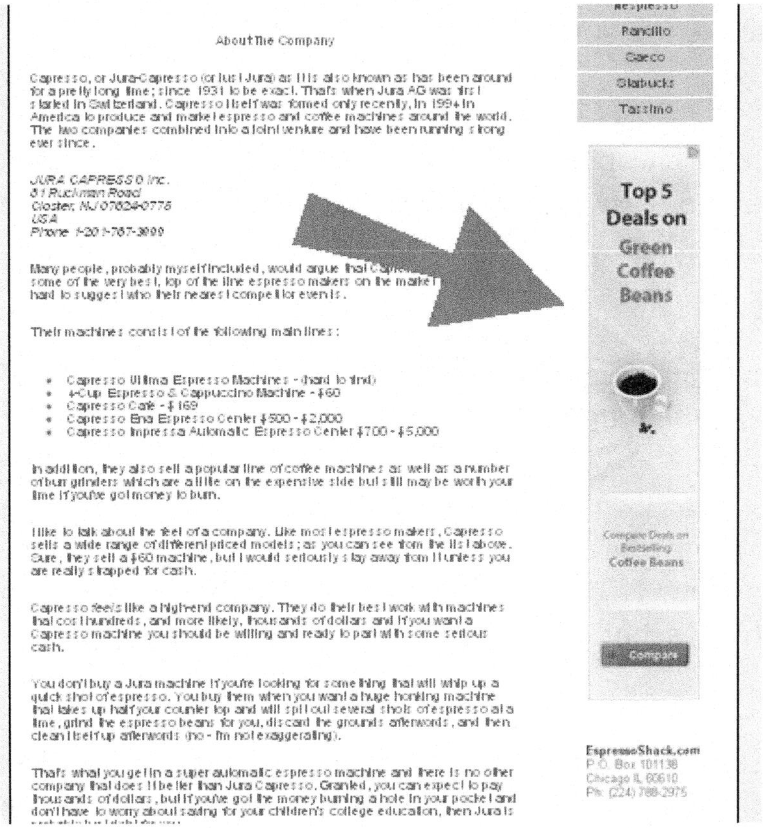

One other tidbit to mention. Notice directly below that ad, you'll see a physical address. That's pretty important because Google like to see addresses these days on web sites.

It really will help your ranking by adding an address to every one of your pages.

Obviously, for privacy reasons, you aren't going to want to use your actual home address.

But it's cheap and easy to get a P.O. Box. But if it's not cheap or easy "enough" for you, then just make up an address.

Who cares, right? It's not like anyone is going to send you stuff in the mail.

Also, on that note, you should also list a telephone number. That's very important for both Google search rankings, but also to just establish credibility.

Again, don't use your actual phone number. People DO call asking all kinds of weird questions. Instead use one of the many free phone number services out there.

I'm talking about Google Voice, or Sipgate, or any of the other services that will give you a totally free phone number and even accept voice mail messages.

It's the perfect solution. People can call in and leave messages and you can listen to those messages straight from your computer.

Win win.

Amazon Affiliate Ads

You'll also notice towards the bottom of every page is a little widget that shows a picture of whatever that page is talking about and a button that you can click to order it directly.

Those are Amazon affiliate ads and they make up a sizeable portion of the income of the site.

Here's a picture of what I'm talking about on the next page:

You'll need to sign up as an affiliate at Amazon.com in order to make money with these ads. You can sign up at: **http://affiliate-program.amazon.com**

There's basically a couple ways to add amazon affiliate offers to your site:

- By Hand

- Using Software Automatically

I prefer to do the second one. I use a neat program called PHPZon that you can check out here: **http://www.marketingfool.com/phpzonrocks.html**

Basically what you do is add a small snippet of code to the bottom of your page and phpzon does the rest. It pulls the picture, price info, and a description straight from amazon and puts it directly on your site like in the picture above.

Phpzon come in a wordpress version and a stand alone api for people like me who hand code their sites with HTML and php.

It's definitely worth the investment. It cost less than a hundred bucks but has brought in untold thousands of dollars in amazon affiliate income to me over the years.

Whenever someone clicks on the "More Details" button like in the picture above, they're transported directly to amazon.com where they can buy the item right then and there.

If they do, you earn a commission of between 6-8% paid out monthly. It's a nice secondary income stream that's not as lucrative as adsense but a very close second place.

Utility Pages

While we're talking about site layout and design, I need to touch upon utility pages.

Utility pages are certain pages that your thick site will absolutely need. These are "About Us", "Contact Us", and "Privacy Policy" pages.

Don't overlook these pages!!

Privacy policy pages are incredibly important because Google adsense (and any legitimate affiliate program you may use like Amazon affiliates) requires that you have a privacy policy in place.

This explains to your site users what you do with the data they may give you, and how you deal with cookies. Since Google adsense ads heavily use cookies, you need to tell your site visitors that.

Failure to have a privacy policy page can get you kicked out of the adsense program. It's no joke.

Fortunately, it doesn't have to be a particularly special privacy policy page, you can use any of the thousands of generic ones floating around on the Internet. Do a Google search if you want.

My privacy policy page is here:
http://espressoshack.marketingfool.com/privacy-policy.html

Feel free to copy it and use it on your own site if you like. In fact, I'll reproduce it here if you want to copy it straight from this eBook, go right ahead.

Just be sure to change the site name from espressoshack.marketingfool.com to your own website's URL!

Privacy Policy

Privacy Policy for espressoshack.marketingfool.com The privacy of the visitors of espressoshack.marketingfool.com is very important to us. At espressoshack.marketingfool.com, we recognize the importance of your specific personal information.

Here is the general information on the types of personal data we receive and collect from you when you visit espressoshack.marketingfool.com, and how we safeguard that data. We will absolutely NEVER sell your personal information or data to any third parties ever. Log files, as with almost any and most web sites, are collected for analytic purposes.

Information in our own log files that we will collect; including your -IP address (Internet Protocol address), and your own ISP Internet Service Provider, and the web browser type that you used to visit espressoshack.marketingfool.com (like Internet Explorer or Firefox or Chrome), and also the time that you visited espressoshack.marketingfool.com and which exact specific web pages you happened to visit throughout espressoshack.marketingfool.com.

espressoshack.marketingfool.com is almost completely advertising supported and while we do not use our own cookies to store information about you, our advertisers just might (including Google via Google Adsense). Information that might or may be stored will include your IP address, and your ISP, and the type of web browser you used when you were visiting espressoshack.marketingfool.com, and in some specific cased whether or not you have the Flash program installed (but not including your name, address, email address, or telephone number).

Google, as a third party vendor, uses cookies to serve ads on our site. Google's use of the DoubleClick DART cookie enables it and its partners to serve ads to you based on your visit to our site and/or other sites on the Internet. You may opt out of the use of the DART cookie by visiting the Google ad and content network privacy policy.

The information that is collected here is generally used for -geotargeting purposes (showing Maine real estate ads to someone in Maine not Texas as one example) or showing certain individual ads based on specific sites visited. These cookies are used mainly to serve ads specific to you and to your specific interests and may be shown based on your own browser history.

You may also choose, on your own, to disable or turn off- selectively those cookies or third party cookies in your web browsers' settings or by managing your own preferences in your own firewall software on your computer. But this can sometimes affect how you can interact with our site(s) and other web sites across the whole internet. This could include not always being able to log into your login sites or services, forums, or even accounts that you are used to loging into.

Subscribing to our

espressoshack.marketingfool.com newsletter: We do not ever rent or sell your specific email address to any third parties of any kind, ever. By subscribing to our newsletter, you will agree to accept email from us in the form of our own special newsletter and any current announcements we may or may not choose to make. You may subscribe or cancel your subscription at any time simply by clicking on a link in any email message that we have sent you which gives you unsubscribe instructions.

These privacy policy terms may be amended or updated by us at any time and it is the duty of you and you alone, the site visitor, to keep current of any amendments or updates by checking back at this page.

Pretty generic, but don't forget to add one to all your thick sites.

SiteMap

It's fairly important to have a sitemap page that has links to all the pages of your site on it. Check out my sitemap page here:
http://espressoshack.marketingfool.com/sitemap.html

You can create an XML sitemap (google it if you don't know what that is) or a regular user-friendly sitemap like the one I listed above.

Or both.

About Us

Don't skimp on the about page either. Really do it up. This is your chance to prove to the Google Quality Reviewers that you're a legitimate website and not some MFA (made for adsense) site.

Tell a story! Explain who you are! Give all your contact info including that fake address and phone number. Heck, in the past I've listed 5-10 fake management employees just to seem like a bigger company than I am.

Just take a look at my About Us Page at:
http://espressoshack.marketingfool.com/about-us.html

> Hello! My name is Jenny and I built this site because I love espresso! My friends know me as the "espresso gal" and they're always asking me

questions about which espresso machine to buy or which coffee beans to use. After a while I decided to just make a web site about it, and EspressoShack.com was born.

I started out writing guides about espresso machines, explaining what they were and how to pick the right one for your needs. That grew into full reviews of specific brands and models. The site exploded from there and now I work on it full time with several people to help me!

So browse around the site. If you have a question about a specific espresso machine that I haven't covered yet, drop me a line! I love talking about this stuff. Also be sure to sign up for my free email newsletter (link above) to get the latest reviews as well as special deals and discounts on some of the leading espresso machines on the market today.

Thanks for coming, and check back soon because I'm always adding new stuff!

-Jenny Alexander
Contact me via **email**
Follow me on **Twitter**

EspressoShack.com
P.O. Box 101138
Chicago, IL 60610
Phone: (224) 788-2975

Obviously my name isn't "Jenny" and my friends don't refer to me as the "Espresso Gal".

But we're building a brand here, and telling a story. All's fair in love and affiliate website building. Have fun with it! It's these little touches that can really add something to a website.

If you're building a model airplane website, maybe brand yourself as a gentle grandfather who loves to work on his model airplanes after retiring from 42 years working for Cessna the airplane company.

Or if you're building a lawn mower website you might be little Timmy the 12 year old boy who mows lawns around the neighborhood and learned so much about the different lawn mowers that he decided to build a website about it.

Whatever, invent something. Turn it into a brand.

And have fun with it.

CHAPTER SIX
Siloing Your Website

Getting traffic from the major search engines, especially Google, is essential for any thick site strategy.

One of the foundations of SEO, or search engine optimization, is siloing a website.

I'm going to talk about SEO in greater detail later, in the search engine ranking chapter, but I wanted to dedicate a whole chapter to the silo so that you know what it's all about and understand the importance of it.

So what is a Silo?

Think of a bunch of grain silo's on a farm. Each silo contains a certain type of thing.

When it comes to a website, the "thing" is content. You don't want to mix the content between silos.

Confused yet? Yeah ok.

Quite simply, each category of your website is a silo, and it should only contain information pertaining to that specific category or silo.

Every one of your web pages should have links to all your categories in the menu on the right hand side of the screen.

But the bottom of each page should have a list of links to the 3-5 (or 10 or 20 or however many pages of content you create per category) pages of content in that category.

It's really a simple concept and once you set up your website to create links like that you never need to think about it again. But it can be a little tricky to wrap your head around it the first time.

If you're using wordpress, then you'll designate each page of content you write by category. You can then install a simple plugin that will put all the links to that specific category at the bottom of each article.

A More Concrete Example

If you're confused, and you should be, maybe we should just go through an example.

Remember back in chapter two where I told you to draw up a roadmap for your site's content? That roadmap is basically your silo structure.

I listed mine, back on page 39-46 or thereabouts. Here's a snippet to jog your memory:

Cuisinart Espresso

- Cuisinart Espresso Machines
- Cuisinart SS-700 Single-Serve Brewing System
- Cuisinart CBM-18 Programmable Conical Burr Mill
- Cuisinart EM-200 Espresso Maker
- Cuisinart EM-100 Espresso Machine

DeLonghi

- DeLonghi Espresso Machines
- DeLonghi BAR32 Retro Pump-Driven 35-ounce Espresso Maker
- DeLonghi EC155 Espresso Maker
- DeLonghi EC702 15-Bar Pump Espresso Maker
- Delonghi EC270 Espresso Machine

Those are basically two **Silos** on my site. The bold words are the silo(Cuisinart Espresso and DeLonghi), the pages listed beneath them are the pages within that silo.

If you check out my site, you'll see that at the bottom of any page within any of those silo's, you'll see links to all the other pages within that silo.

That's siloing.

That's it.

It's a way to group information that Google really likes to see and you should go out of your way to build your sites in this fashion because it'll go a long way in getting you great search engine traffic.

But even better, it's a helpful way for people to find specific information on your site.

If someone comes to your website looking for information on a DeLonghi EC155 Espresso Maker and reads the article you've written about it, they may be likely to want to also read about the DeLonghi EC702 15-Bar Pump Espresso Maker - and will - if they see a link to it at the bottom of the page after reading the first article.

So it's helpful to people, it's helpful to the search engines, and it's generally just a good practice all the way around.

If you're using wordpress, there are free plugins that you can use to silo your site by category. Just make sure to set up your wordpress categories as the different categories of your niche and you'll be fine.

You can just hunt around a little on the interwebs to find those plugins. Any will work as long as they slap your silo links at the bottom of each page within that silo.

In fact, wordpress was really designed to compliment this structure, it's almost built into wordpress itself.

There are more than one way to silo a website, this is just the way that I like to use and it seems to work best for me, but you don't necessarily have to stick to that form.

Some people like to do a hard silo, where they'll actually put each silo in its own directory.

For instance instead of the URL:

http://espressoshack.marketingfool.com/Cuisinart-EM-200-Espresso-Maker.html

(Which is the structure I use) They would use something like this:

http://espressoshack.marketingfool.com/Cuisinart/Cuisinart-EM-200-Espresso-Maker.html

Notice the difference? There's a /Cuisinart/ directory there.

http://espressoshack.marketingfool.com/**Cuisinart**/Cuisinart-EM-200-Espresso-Maker.html

That's a hard or physical silo. Wordpress will often do that, and that's fine.

However you decide to silo doesn't really matter. It's really just a matter of style.

Siloing is a very basic concept in SEO (search engine optimization) so if you're still a little fuzzy on the concept after reading this chapter, you can Google it and read up on it in more detail.

The important takeaway from this chapter is that you need to structure your website in an intelligent way so that it's easy to categorize for Google and easy to navigate for your site visitors.

Siloing is a great place to start.

CHAPTER SEVEN
Ranking Your Site At Google

Ranking your thick site well at Google is both important and not important.

Everyone wants a good ranking so that you'll get a ton of traffic, but I did very little to no SEO work on my espresso shack website and it earned a nice amount of money.

But I understand the desire for people to boost their ranking and therefore boost their income.

In my opinion though, you'd be much better off spending your time building another site than working on the SEO of an old site.

I'd rather have 2 websites that earned $3,000 each ($6,000 total) than 1 website that earned $4,500 after I did a bunch of SEO work on it.

Not to mention the fact that Google is CONSTANTLY changing their algorithm and constantly changing the rules of the game as far as SEO is concerned.

What might have been perfectly acceptable SEO behavior last month can get you banned from Google the next month. You just never know.

I much rather take a natural approach to SEO for thick sites. (now THIN sites is a whole other story!).

As a result of this philosophy, during the recent mad Google changes (known in the industry as the penguin update and the panda update) my thick sites have remained relatively unscathed, whereas my thin sites got decimated across the board.

So what SHOULD you do, SEO wise?

The beauty of my thick site strategy is that it is powerfully seo'd from the start.

If you build your site in the method I've laid out (silo'd based on categories, categories based on brands, etc) then your site is already naturally seo'd beautifully.

You do want to focus on a few things on the individual page level that I'm going to talk about right now, namely:

- Description and Keyword Meta Tags
- Page Titles
- Keywords in the page content itself
- Silos

Let's go through each of those things.

Description Meta Tags

If you've been in the world of SEO very long, you don't need me to explain description meta tags.

Basically they're a short little synopsis of your page, 150-180 characters or so long that you put into a little meta tag at the top of each of your pages.

It should describe exactly what's on that page, and that page only.

The actual meta tag looks like this:

<meta name="description" content="Cuisinart espresso machines are great espresso makers for the price. Don't spend more than you have to - get them on sale today right here.">

And that goes between your page's <head> and </head> html tag.

That meta tag came from this page:
http://espressoshack.marketingfool.com/cuisinart.html

If you're using wordpress, I suggest you download the "all in one seo pack" which is a free plugin that allows you to enter your meta tag data directly when creating a post.

Many times Google will take your description meta tag and use it as the description for your Search Engine Result at Google.

So keep that in mind and try to write something that:

1. Has your pages main keyword listed in it once.

2. Is compelling enough to convince someone to visit your site.

Keyword Meta Tag

The keyword tag is much like the description tag, except it lists 5-10 of the keywords pertaining to your particular web page.

Most search engines ignore that tag these days, but you never know so you should use it.

Here's an example of a keyword meta tag, again from the same

http://espressoshack.marketingfool.com/cuisinart.html

page.

<meta name="keywords" content="Cuisinart espresso machines, cuisinart espresso makers, EM-100, EM-200, Cuisinart EM-100, Cuisinart EM-200, Cuisinart Coffee Bean Grinder">

Don't go overboard, just list the pages main keyword, then a few variations of that main keyword.

Or for your category pages, list the main keywords for all the pages within that category.

A Few Words On Keywords...

What is the main keyword of your page? It's the word or phrase that you most want to get listed under at Google for that particular page.

In our case, it's going to be the title of the page as listed in the roadmap back from chapter two.

Here's a snippet from my roadmap:

Cuisinart Espresso

- Cuisinart Espresso Machines
- Cuisinart SS-700 Single-Serve Brewing System
- Cuisinart CBM-18 Programmable Conical Burr Mill
- Cuisinart EM-200 Espresso Maker
- Cuisinart EM-100 Espresso Machine

Each of those is a particular page of your website and therefore the main keyword of that page.

So on the Cuisinart Espresso Machines page, your main keyword would be "Cuisinart Espresso Machines".

For the Cuisinart EM-200 Espresso Maker pages, the main keyword would be "Cuisinart EM-200 Espresso Maker".

You get the idea.

That leads us to the next item on our list…

Page Titles

This one's pretty easy. Each title for each page should be that page's keyword. The same keyword we just discussed.

The title should be used in two places on each page.

1. The page's html <title> tag

2. Actually on the page right above the main adsense ad block.

If you aren't familiar with HTML then you won't know what the <title> tag is, but it's very similar to the meta tags I just talked about.

It goes between your pages <head> and </head> tag and looks like this, again taken from this example page: **http://espressoshack.marketingfool.com/cuisinart.html**

<title>Cuisinart Espresso Machines | Find the best Deals!</title>

If you're using wordpress, you don't need to worry about this because wordpress will slap the title into the <title> tag automatically based on whatever title you give each page.

The next place to put your title is directly above the main adsense ad block on each page.

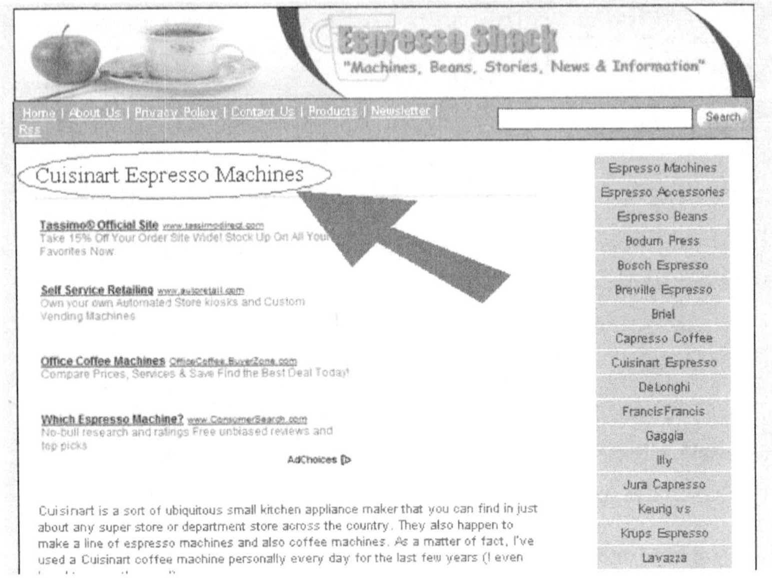

Pretty straight forward. Don't elaborate, don't try and be fancy, just use the exact keyword from your roadmap.

Keywords in the page content itself

Next, you're going to want to use the page's main keyword within the content of the page itself, but don't over-do it!

I try to use it 2-3 times in a 500 word article and maybe another time or so if the article is 1,000 to 1,200 words long.

You can use the word singularly, or plural (plurally?). ie, if your main keyword is Cuisinart Espresso Machines, you could write it as the plural or singular form. For instance:

> *We've always used Cuisinart Espresso Machines in our house and always will because they're solid and dependable.*
>
> *I went to all the major stores in the area, but they were all so overpriced that I eventually went online to amazon.com (if you can believe it!) and ordered my Cuisinart Espresso Machine straight from them. Books and espresso machines, I guess it does make a certain sort of sense!*

See what I did there? I highlighted the keyword in red to make a point (don't do that on your actual website). But you can see how you might weave your keyword into the content of your page.

Again, I can't stress this enough, don't over-do it!

Use your keyword just a few times at the most in each article you write, otherwise Google will just determine that you're trying to spam them with keyword stuffing.

Plus it isn't a very pleasant reading experience for a site visitor to have to keep reading the phrase Cuisinart Espresso Machines over and over and over and over again.

Siloing

I talked about silo'ing in the last chapter so I won't go into in further here, but it's a very important part of natural SEO so I at least wanted to mention it.

Is That It?

Really that's all I did for my espresso shack website and the results were quite satisfactory.

But I acknowledge that other people may want more, so I do have a few more tips. These tips range from what I'd call "good natural SEO" to "more risky SEO".

Directories

Directories have long been a tool for the SEO professional, but most SEO types get it wrong and just submit websites to tons of major directories.

That's the wrong way to do it.

You want to focus on micro niche directories that pertain ONLY to whatever your website is about.

For instance, I once owned a radio controlled airplane website (before I sold it on flippa).

As you might expect, there are a lot of hobby type websites pertaining to RC Airplanes, and some of them have little directories or even just lists of other RC Airplane related sites.

I spent a long afternoon once searching for a bunch of these websites and contacting the owners, either by email or phone if they listed a phone number.

I explained that I had a new RC airplane site and I'd like to get it listed in their directory or list.

Many of them had submission forms that you could fill out for inclusion, which is great.

To make a long and boring story short, I got my site listed in a few of them.

You'd be amazed how much traffic that generated. Initially it pulled in a nice amount of traffic from the directories themselves, but eventually Google took notice too and gave me a really solid boost to my rankings.

Google loves social proof…especially these days… so if the Radio Controlled community decides your RC site is good enough to list in their directories, Google does too.

LinkBait

Linkbait is another powerful natural SEO method. What you do is create a report, podcast, bit of software, set of recipes, whatever that people who visit your site might be interested.

Then you give it away for free in exchange for a link to your web site.

You can do it explicitly or implicitly. By that I mean you can force people to give you a link in exchange for your freebie, or you can just hope that people will like it so much that they'll link to it and tell their friends.

Both ways can work.

This is a great method because it's viral and exponential and works forever without any extra work on your part. Once you create the thing, your work is done.

People will then find it themselves and pass it on themselves.

And it's easy with these niche type sites. I didn't do it for espressoshack.com but I could easily have created a special report called:

"The beginners guide to buying your first espresso machine"

Or something like that. Then just write a little 20-50 page ebook teaching people what to look for in their first espresso machine.

Esspresso machines confuse people at first, a free guide like that might have been really helpful.

And the great thing is; you're an expert. You just got done writing 100-150 articles about your niche, so you know virtually everything you could possibly need to know in order to write a neat little free report like that.

Social Media

Get people to follow your site on facebook and twitter and start sending out weekly deals tweets or facebook status updates.

Amazon.com affiliate items are always going on sale. If I took a look around their site each week and grabbed a couple of sale items and then announced it through twitter or facebook (along with my affiliate links so that if they click on it and buy, I get a commission), I bet people would like to see that.

There are a zillion things you can do with social media that are beyond the scope of this eBook, but keep it in mind.

Traditional SEO

Traditional SEO, in my mind, is risky these days and that's why I suggest you stay away from it.

Historically you would do a lot of social bookmarking and un-natural link building to boost your ranking.

But these days Google frowns on all of that so harshly, that it's almost dangerous to even try.

One tip that I WILL give you if you absolutely MUST stray into this gray area is this:

Go Slowly!

Whatever you do, do it slowly. Don't build links too quickly, don't post to social bookmarking sites too quickly, don't submit tons of articles to article marketing directories too quickly.

Slow and steady is the name of the game with Google. You want to make your SEO actions look as natural as possible.

That's all I'll say on the subject. You can do your own research and take your own chances if you want to stray off further in this area.

CHAPTER EIGHT
Selling Your Sites

So we've pretty much gone over everything you need to build your thick website and now we need to talk about selling them, specifically on flippa.com (the leading auction site for selling websites).

There's a ton of things involved in selling a web site, and I could really write and entire eBook on that alone…in fact, I might just do that in the future.

But I want to give you as much info as you'll need to get the job done.

So let's just dive right in!

When To Sell Your Site…

There is no one size fits all answer when it comes to selling sites, but there are several useful guidelines that you can use.

Personally, I like to build in a pre-set time period for selling a website whenever I build a site.

That is, as soon as I build it, I'm already thinking about selling it. It's not something I just decide to do one day out of the blue. It's all part of the overall profit strategy of the site.

As a general rule, I like to sell sites at around the 10 month mark. Why? I don't know; that's just sort of what I've come up with over the years.

These days sites sell for around 10 times their monthly earnings. So if you have 10 months of those earnings, and they're all pretty much steady and equal, you're going to have a good baseline on what to charge.

Not only that, but you'll have a nice amount of earnings "proof" for the buyer.

I mean, you can sell a site after just 2-3 months of earnings to show, and I've seen people do that often.

But think of it from the buyer's point of view. If you were going to spend thousands of dollars on a website, would you feel more comfortable if the site had 10 months of steady earnings that you could look at, or only 2 or 3 months of earnings?

But One Size Does Not Fit All!

That's not to say that you shouldn't sell a site earlier! If you had 3 months of rocket earnings followed by a fourth month of plummeted earnings, you might want to try to sell it before more bad earnings roll in.

So it just depends.

But as a general rule, I like to shoot for 10 months.

Why Not Just Keep Them?

Sometimes I do, but I like to always sell a percentage of my sites no matter what, and it's a high percentage.

I'll probably sell 75% of all my thick sites unless they're just REALLY going strong.

The problem is - the Internet is a fluid beast. Who knows what Google will do in the future, who knows what people will like in the future.

Some new technology might come out, some new wordpress alternative, or mobile alternative that makes your site look old and outdated.

In my mind, it's better to always be building new sites with new looks and feels, all the while slowly and systematically selling off your old ones.

That's why I set a built in timer to sell my sites after 10 months.

Plus, I'd rather have the equivalent of next years entire earnings in my pocket today than wait around for them to dribble in month by month over the next year.

I studied finance and economics in college, believe me – it's better to have the full amount now vs small bits over time. It's a concept called the time-value of money.

Normally you would discount future earnings to present dollars, but that doesn't happen when you sell your site at flippa so you come out ahead in real dollars.

But that's all beyond the scope of this eBook and I'm getting off track.

Think of it like this...say you'd like to always have 50 sites. That's a nice manageable number.

After you build the 50 sites, say over the course of 10 months (or whatever) then you start selling them in order, ie you'd start selling the first site you built, then the second...say one every week.

Then you'd also build a new web site at the same time. So you're always selling one, and building one...so your total portfolio of websites stays at 50.

Costs are another consideration. Every year you'll have to renew your domain name and it'll cost you $10-12 per domain (and that price is only going to go up as the years go by).

That might not seem like a lot of money, but if you've got 50 sites, that's $500-600 a year in domain registration fees!

Imagine if you owned 100 websites! You're looking at $1,000-$1,200 a year in domain registration fees.

That can really take a bite out of your overall profits. If you sell those sites before the year is up, you don't have to pay those domain registration fees.

Sure, you still have to pay the fee's to register the domain of the new site that you build to replace it, but domain registrars like Godaddy will often run special low price deals for new domain registrations.

Sometimes as low as $1 to $5.99 depending on how diligent you are. At my special **MarketingFool.com Members-Only** website we always keep an eye out for sales and pass that info along to our members.

The savings you get right there almost pays for your MarketingFool.com Members-Only Membership alone!

But I'm getting off the topic again.

How Much To Charge

The first thing to do is determine how much to sell your site for.

Flippa is an auction site, but you still have some control over the price you'll accept.

There are several mechanisms that you can use, from listing a BIN price (Buy It Now) to listing a minimum that you won't accept less than.

Typically I won't ever set a minimum, and I'll accept $1 for a site. That gets the ball rolling and the bidding never stays that low for long.

As I mentioned earlier, sites typically bring in around 10 times their monthly average earnings. If you have 10 months of earnings, this is easy to calculate.

Be sure to factor in all forms of income, from Adsense earnings, to Amazon affiliate earnings, and anything else you might have.

Before I get into the details of selling a site, why don't you head over to Flippa.com and check out the listing for my espressoshack.com website.

You can find it here: **https://flippa.com/2743371-1-500-earnings-pr4-espresso-authority-website-great-content-multiple-revenues**

Yes, the seller is listed as Jennifer77 but that's me. I knew I was going to use this website as a case study so I used an anonymous flippa account so that my other sales would remain a secret.

You probably don't want to do that yourself, you want people to know who you are and be able to see your history. It builds trust and makes it easier to sell sites.

Plus you'll gain a following if you're there for a while. Serious buyers will know to keep an eye on you and your auctions.

Plus people may come to trust your work so much (after several successful sales) that they may contact you outside of flippa to buy your sites direct.

That sort of thing happens all the time and is great, because that way you don't have to pay the sometimes expensive flippa fee's.

So take a look at that listing. Please feel free to copy it completely when selling your sites. Just swap out the information I provided with your own info.

Check it out…

Notice the description…again, I'm telling a story, much like I did in the "About" page of the website. Selling is story-telling, it always has been and always will be. Make it compelling.

After a little bit of story telling, I dive right into the details. The more numbers you can give, the stronger your sale will be.

If the site has a high Google page rank, list that. If it has a high number of pages indexed in Google, list that. Whatever you can think of to add data is good.

Take a look at the title:

$1,500 Earnings PR4 Espresso Authority Website - Great Content Multiple Revenues

I like to start right out by listing the earnings. That's what people really care about, so grab their attention.

Take a look at the right hand side of the screen. There's a section called "attachments".

That's where you upload analytics information and earnings information. I like to take snapshots of adsense earnings and post them there (though I believe flippa now has a system to verify adsense earnings independently).

Again, the more information you can provide the better.

Flippa Fee's

Flippa isn't free, and it's not really all that cheap either. But it's definitely worth it.

The main fee to list a site is (at the time of writing) $29. That's not really all that bad when you get right down to it.

After that you can expect to pay 5% of the sale price. So if your site sells for $1,000 you would then owe flippa $50 and they'll charge your credit card automatically for that amount.

There is a $2,000 cap fee on that 5%. So if your site sells for $2 million dollars, you only owe $2,000.

I believe you can set the auction up so that the buyer pays the 5% success fee, or you split it. That's really up to you.

Further, if you choose to use escrow.com (which I highly recommend over paypal) then you're going to incur some fee's there as well.

Again, like the success fee, you can designate that the buyer pays all or some of that fee. You just have to spell that out in your auction listing so that the potential buyer understands going in that they're going to be responsible for those fees.

There's a bunch of other things that you can pay for at flippa as well; things like:

- Listing featured on the front page $50
- Hide listing completely from public view $30
- Listing title in bold $5
- Listing row highlighted $10
- Screenshot on listing row $20
- Hide from search engines and non-logged in users $20
- Tweet listing to @flippa followers $80
- Premium Domain Listing $500
- Premium Website Listing $250

And probably some others as well. I've never paid for any of those things, and I've never had trouble selling a website.

Believe me, if you've got a solid, established website with dozens or hundreds of pages of content that's bringing in steady earnings month after month, you're not going to have a hard time selling your site.

And you won't have to pay for any of those extra bells and whistles to do it.

Get To Know Flippa

Spend a lot of time reading all the frequently asked questions and tutorials at flippa, both for buying as well as selling websites.

Spend time browsing through other listings. Take special note of the ones that sell for a lot of money and the ones that tank. What makes them different?

Especially keep an eye out for other adsense type sites like yours. If you see someone selling a lot of them, follow their auctions more closely.

The more you learn about the whole flippa process, the easier its going to be to sell your sites and the more money you'll ultimately make.

So a little research can go a long way here, especially when we're talking about selling sites for thousands of dollars.

One Caveat

One thing to look out for is paypal. NEVER accept payment via paypal.

I know its super easy to use paypal, but you've really got to resist the urge. I've heard horror stories from people who've used paypal to accept payment for website sales and I've even experienced one myself.

Here's what can happen.

Someone bids on your site and wins, then pays you with paypal. You transfer the website to them as well as the domain name.

You no longer have anything, they've got it all.

Now they initiate a chargeback at paypal and claim that they never received the item.

Paypal considers websites and domain names to be digital items and will, as a matter of policy, side with the buyer on all digital chargeback or refund issues.

They'll then refund the buyers money in full immediately and there's nothing you can do about it. There is no recourse, there is nothing you can do.

Unless you've physically mailed them a physical product, paypal will refund their money no questions asked. You can't even appeal.

And now you no longer have your website either.

This is a common scam that's been around for a while, but it's not the only problem you can run into with paypal.

People have buyers remorse, especially for big ticket items. They spend a couple thousand dollars on your site and then a month later something comes up and they need some money.

A quick email to paypal and they can get their purchase refunded no questions asked. It's a huge problem.

I've had that happen to me before once.

I've also had someone demand a refund because the site didn't earn as much money as they thought it would.

Granted, they changed the site around, removed a bunch of stuff, changed the structure and graphics, and took 2 months to get the site setup after I had given it to them.

In the mean time, Google saw an empty site sitting there for 2 months and basically dropped it off the face of the cliff in the search engine results (like duh, of course they'd do that if the site virtually disappeared).

By the time the new owner got around to putting the site back up, they were mystified that it no longer had a decent Google ranking and wanted their money back.

Again, it would have been easy for them to get their money back if we'd used paypal…fortunately by then I had learned my lesson and now only use escrow.com.

My point is; be careful. We're talking about a lot of money and people will do some pretty skuzzy things when large amounts of money are at stake.

Escrow.com is a perfect solution. It doesn't cost much and they will hold the buyers money and your website in escrow themselves until the conditions of the sale are met, and then they'll release them to each party.

It's great.

And you can even designate that the buyer pays all escrown.com fee's when you put your site up for sale.

CHAPTER NINE

Putting It All Together

So there you have it! At the end of the day, the strategy isn't very difficult; it's just a matter of creating a plan and following through.

It may seem daunting at first, but the trick is to just start with one website.

Work on it as much as you can, but don't stress it if you have problems. Slow and steady is fine when you're first starting out.

Just get that one website built. Because once you start to see money role in, even if it's just a dollar or two a day, you'll have huge motivation to grow and expand your empire.

After you SEE that the strategy works with your first site, then it's much easier to push forward with future sites.

Plus building that first site costs virtually no money. You basically need like $8 to register the domain, and $20 for the first month's Hostgator web hosting.

And if you don't want to hand code your sites with html and php like I do, expect to pay another $17 for the clickbump wordpress engine and another $15 for his theme that looks like my sites.

Total investment…around $60.

What other full fledged business can you start for $60? I can't think of a single one really. That's what makes this so powerful and intriguing for so many people.

You'll probably make mistakes at first. You might pick a bad niche or write bad articles or something else.

IT DOESN'T MATTER!

Just go out and do it! You'll learn from your mistakes and move on. In no time at all you'll be a pro at this, I have no doubt.

And there's help out there if you need it. My Member's Only website is a great place to start. In the appendix at the end of this book I'll give you a really good discounted price on my member's only website as a thank you for purchasing this book.

You can read more about it in the appendix...but basically it comes to literally pennies a day (and not many pennies at that!) to get all the help and support you could ever need.

I highly recommend you check it out (it comes with a no questions asked money back guarantee so you have nothing to lose).

I've seen the same thing happen time and time again. People pour a ton of time and effort into building a website and then don't see results because they've done something slightly wrong.

It's easy to take one very quick look at their work and see what the problem is and show them how to fix it in a matter of minutes.

That sort of hands on help and advice is really invaluable.

Not to mention that Google and Adsense are constantly changing. What works today might not work exactly as planned tomorrow.

Part of what our community does is keep an eye out for changes and adapt accordingly. We share what's working and what's not working with each other so that we can all stay ahead of the game.

It's really great and I can't speak highly enough about it. So check it out at **www.marketingfool.com/member** if you're even a little interested.

The Final Blueprint...

So here's a final blueprint or checklist of the overall strategy for you to refer back to.

1. Pick a broad product niche
2. Research and create a list of 20-30 brands within that niche (usually using Amazon.com)
3. Create a list of 5-10 products for each brand (usually using amazon.com and the free keyword tool).
4. Create your site blueprint using the brands and products you've researched in the previous steps.
5. Register a domain name.

6. Set up your webhosting.

7. If using wordpress, install your wordpress theme.

8. Start cranking out articles about each item in your site blueprint until the site is done.

9. Possibly do some natural SEO work (but not much).

10. Rinse and repeat for the next website!

It seems really easy…and in a lot of ways…it is! Thanks for reading my eBook. I hope you enjoyed it as much as I enjoyed writing it for you.

And I hope to see you at my Member's Only website.

Until then….

KEEP ON BUILDING!!

-John Elder
The Marketing Fool!

APPENDIX ONE

Members Only…

Throughout this whole eBook I've mentioned several times my special Member's-Only website.

It's a place where you can get hands on help with your Adsense Empire, take part in our vibrant Adsense community, interact with other like-minded Internet Marketers, and get a ton of other tools and information to help grow your business.

www.marketingfool.com/member

As a special thank you for purchasing this eBook, I'd like to extend a very special discount offer on membership.

I think my membership site is one of the best resources on the Internet for both Adsense and Internet Marketing in general.

We've got people there who have done it all…made buckets of money, and have years of experience; and they're all willing to share their knowledge.

So in my mind, any price is worth it; especially since it comes with a no questions asked money back guarantee.

Membership usually costs $27 a month, or $299 a year. But as a special thank you for being a past customer of mine, I'm offering you a special discount price of just:

$99 for one year's membership

There is a string attached though. I only allow 100 members at any one time. I like to keep the number down so that I can make sure that absolutely everyone is able to get the hands on help that they need.

What that means is that if you're interested in that special $99 discount deal, you need to act now while there's spots available.

To order now, go to:
www.marketingfool.com/member-special

There you can find a link to a secure order form page. If the order form page is up, that means there's spots left and you can order.

If the order form page is down, then unfortunately you didn't move fast enough. I do keep a mailing list that you can sign up for to notify people when a new spot opens though.

I do apologize if this seems like an artificial marketing ploy, it's really not. In the past I've been a part of membership sites that had over 100 people in them, and the quality of the site really dropped after around the 100 mark.

And that's not fair to anyone. It's my goal to create the most helpful members-only adsense site on the Internet, so I think it's really important to keep it small and agile. 100 is the perfect number.

What You Get?

Membership comes with quite a lot of benefits.

1. Free eBooks and Software

First, you get a copy of every MarketingFool.com eBook or tool that I write or create, for free.

I'm always writing new eBooks on different exciting Adsense things. Any time I do, you get it free while everyone else has to pay full price.

That includes software too. I'm a programmer, and I'm always building cool little tools like my Quick Index Tool. As a member you get them all free too.

2. ***Member's-Only Message Board***

You get access to the actual member's only message board where we sit around and discuss everything you could possibly think of relating to Adsense, and Internet Marketing, and everything else.

Share what's working for you, see what's working for others. Ask questions, read what other people have asked over time, and on and on.

It's a great hub filled with like minded people all interested in one thing…making as much money online as possible!

3. ***Case Studies***

I'm always building different types of sites, from thick sites to thin sites to shopping sites, to ecommerce sites, to price comparison sites and on and on.

I like to journal these different sites and walk people through them step by step, and you get access to all of that as a member.

Right now as I write this, I'm building a new super price comparison site and shopping engine. It's really cool, and

I'm showing my members exactly how I'm doing it, how much money it's making, etc etc.

This is a great way to expand your own Adsense Empire by watching me, seeing what works, and copying it.

I'll also often give you templates so that you can make these sites even easier.

4. Special Offers

From time to time the members of our group might find a special tool out on the Internet that we especially like. When that happens I'll contact the company and try to negotiate a special discount just for us.

Hey, companies love to give discounts for potential mass orders and there are nearly 100 of us at any given time. So it works out for every one.

5. And More…

It's a vibrant community and it's growing and evolving as it goes along. We're still relatively new, so now's your chance to really get in on the ground floor (so to speak).

I recommend that you don't wait, order today to lock in a year's membership at just $99.

And remember that it comes with a no questions asked money back guarantee. I'm not happy if you aren't happy, and I won't squabble about it like some people will. I'll just refund your money and thank you for giving it a try!

Order here:
www.marketingfool.com/member-special

APPENDIX TWO
Resources…

Throughout this book I've mentioned several different resources, so I thought it'd be a good idea to list them all here so that you have easy access to them and don't have to hunt around the book to look them up.

EspressoShack.com Example Site:
http://espressoshack.marketingfool.com

Username: espresso
Password: shack

Godaddy Domain Names Discount:
http://www.MarketingFool.com/godaddyrocks.html

Hostgator Web Hosting:
http://www.MarketingFool.com/hostgatorrocks.html

Servint Web Hosting:
http://www.MarketingFool.com/servintrocks.html

ClickBump WordPress Themes:
http://www.MarketingFool.com/clickbumprocks.html

PhpZon Amazon Affiliate Widget:
http://www.MarketingFool.com/phpzonrocks.html

MarketingFool.com Members-Only Website:
http://www.marketingfool.com/member

Special MarketingFool.com Members-Only Discount:
http://www.marketingfool.com/member-special

Flipp Website Auction:
http://www.Flippa.com

My EspressoShack.com Flippa Listing:
https://flippa.com/2743371-1-500-earnings-pr4-espresso-authority-website-great-content-multiple-revenues

Amazon.com Affiliate Program website:
http://affiliate-program.amazon.com

BestSpinner Software:
http://www.MarketingFool.com/bestspinnerrocks.html

Article Builder Software:
http://www.MarketingFool.com/articlebuilderrocks.html

THE END

All material contained in this book is for informational purposes only and is no substitute for professional advice. Neither John Elder, MarketingFool.com, Flatplanet Media, LLC or it's affiliates (collectively referred to as COMPANY) make any guarantees of the tactics or strategies described in this book. Successful use of any tactic or strategy described in this book depends on the specific person, their experience, and their business and marketing ability. COMPANY makes no claims or guarantees regarding income generated from the use of any tactic or strategy described in this book. Reader agrees to indemnify and hold COMPANY harmless from and against any and all claims, demands, liabilities, expenses, losses, damages, attorney fees arising from any and all claims and lawsuits for libel, slander, copyright, and trademark violation as well as all other claims resulting from reading this book. Adsense is a registered trademark of Google.

Printed in Dunstable, United Kingdom

91218886R00107